GHOSTS OF THE
SOUTH CAROLINA
UPCOUNTRY

GHOSTS OF THE SOUTH CAROLINA UPCOUNTRY

TALLY JOHNSON

Haunted
America

Published by Haunted America
A Division of The History Press
Charleston, SC 29403
www.historypress.net

Copyright © 2005 by Talmadge Johnson
All rights reserved

Cover Image: Old abandoned plantation owner's home near Monticello, South Carolina.
Courtesy the Library of Congress.

First published 2005
Second printing 2007
Third printing 2012

Manufactured in the United States

978.1.59629.057.0

Library of Congress Cataloging-in-Publication Data

Johnson, Talmadge.
Ghosts of the South Carolina upcountry / Talmadge Johnson.
p. cm.
Includes bibliographical references.
ISBN 1-59629-057-9 (alk. paper)
1. Haunted places--South Carolina. 2. Ghosts--South Carolina. 3. South
Carolina--History. I. Title.
BF1472.U6J655 2005
133.1'09757'2--dc22
2005022250

CONTENTS

ACKNOWLEDGEMENTS

To my parents, Mike and Doris Johnson, for always encouraging me to try everything; to my wife Rachel, for putting up with a house full of books and a husband with ghosts on the brain; to my friends and extended family, for their support and willingness to drive all over while I bored them to tears with the same old stories; to my colleagues in both the history and library/archives fields, for their assistance; and to Nancy and Bruce Roberts, for blazing the trail and planting the seed for this book.

PREFACE

This book will not meet your expectations—especially if you are used to folk tales in dialect, highly technical descriptions of various "ghost-busting" tools and a steadily serious tone. None of those things will be found here. Instead you will find ghostlore from thirteen different counties in Upstate South Carolina. I will intersperse some history (as befits my background and my publisher), but I feel the stories say more about the mindset of the people involved than any plain factual narrative.

I myself am of two minds about ghosts and their existence. I believe ghosts exist, having seen several and experienced more, but all are not the remnants of a dead person or animal back from the grave for some great purpose like revenge or to find happiness. Most ghosts can best be described as short snippets of video from the past, with an occasional interaction with the present tossed in for variety. Most ghosts or hauntings occur without any intention of influencing the living. However, a few, like the Hound of Goshen found in Union and Newberry Counties, do interact with the living. One of my favorite pastimes is going on impromptu ghost hunts with friends. Most, if not all, of the sites in this book have been visited in this manner over the years.

The time period covered by this book ranges in theory from the late 1500s to the 1970s, though, sadly, the earliest story has no real background in either local lore or history. All of the sites mentioned are at least publicly accessible; though some sites are private residences and may not be open to guests. When in doubt, contact the local chamber of commerce or public library to clarify a site's status.

Finally, a word about the tone of the book: do not expect it to be dry or constantly serious. One of my outreach tools in my job at the Chester County Library is to go to area schools and other libraries and tell ghost stories. My format is unusual, however. I ask the students to give a place, preferably a general one like "a theater" or "a shopping mall," and then I tell a story with that setting. Most of these tales have been gathered by my reading, but many are based on personal experience. I cannot do any dialect but a Southern one, so I don't use "funny voices" in my appearances, and I won't use any dialect in print, as I find it to be hard to read and a distraction. I try to keep things light during my shows since many ghost stories deal with murder, betrayal and other sensitive topics. Of course, having seen enough horror movies to know that a joke cuts the tension enough for the next scare to be good, I'm not above copying that technique.

So, sit back, dim the lights and enjoy. If you find yourself in Chester, or Spartanburg or Newberry one day, take a side trip and check out one of the sites mentioned. As I tell the kids after a particularly gruesome tale, "Wouldn't it be cool to see it yourself? Let me know how it goes…"

Author's Note: All accounts and events in this book are related as they occurred to the people involved. The author has sought to verify all personal accounts with other sources, but in some cases, that was not possible. The author also states that the events in this book are true to the best of his knowledge. Any location where the author failed to have an experience may still be haunted, but some people are luckier than others.

ANDERSON COUNTY

Anderson County is located in the northwest corner of South Carolina. It is bordered by the state of Georgia, and Oconee, Pickens, Greenville and Abbeville Counties. Anderson County was first settled by the English in the mid-1750s, though the Cherokees and other tribes had of course been there long before. A Spanish explorer named Juan Pardo passed through the area in about 1540 with part of the De Soto expedition, but no settlement followed. White settlement was slowed by the Native American presence, which mounted several vicious campaigns culminating in the Snow Campaign of 1775. This series of battles led to a treaty in 1777 that effectively ended "Indian Territory" in South Carolina and started an incipient land rush, sped along by the large numbers of Revolutionary veterans claiming bounty land grants.

Only one Revolutionary battle was fought in what is now Anderson County, however. Anderson County was formed in 1826 from part of the Pendleton District. The new county was named for Robert Anderson, an early settler and veteran of the Revolution. As the nineteenth century passed, Anderson County played a role in every American war, especially by supplying manpower to the Confederacy. A Civil War skirmish was fought in the county on May 1, 1865, between cadets en route to Newberry to be discharged and a band of Stoneman's Raiders. No injuries or fatalities were reported.

Anderson County can lay claim to three governors of South Carolina: James Orr, Olin Johnston and George B. Timmerman Jr.; as well as Confederate General Barnard Bee, who gave General Thomas Jackson his nickname of "Stonewall" at First Bull Run before being fatally wounded. Jim Rice, longtime all-star outfielder and American League MVP for the Boston Red Sox, is also a native of Anderson County. The city of Anderson was one of the first cities to use high-voltage hydropower commercially, in 1897.

The first version of the cry baby bridge

I truly believe every county has at least one "cry baby bridge." Of course, most accounts don't inspire award-winning mystery authors like Mignon Ballard to base novels on them. Her novel *Cry at Dusk*, a modern-day Gothic tale set in rural South Carolina, is said to reveal the true tale of the haunted bridge near the intersection of High Shoals Road and Broadway Lake Road near Pine Lake Golf Club southeast of Anderson, South Carolina.

According to local legend, a mother and child went out for a drive. In one version of the tale, the mother has a wreck and both mother and baby are killed. The ghostly after-effects in this version include witnesses being able to watch the car still attempt to cross the bridge—it never makes it—and hearing the cries of the baby in the background.

Ballard's version is slightly different:

> On certain nights you can hear the baby crying, see its tiny form being swept beneath the bridge in an eddy of fog.

Even still, there is no reason given for this desperate act.

Strange happenings at the Sullivan Building

The story of the haunting at the Sullivan Building at Anderson College is one of the most often told of the Upstate's ghost stories. However, the college denies that any of its buildings are haunted. The haunting has been reported in many different places, including a book by Nancy Roberts and an article in the *Anderson Independent-Mail* newspaper. Oddly, though the college denies that the haunting ever happened or has any basis in fact, an article even appeared in the college newsletter, *Echoes*.

The Sullivan Building on the campus of Anderson College has a long history. It was built between 1911 and 1924 and added to the National Register of Historic Places with the rest of the campus in 1998. It has served as the school president's house and the music building and is currently the home to the Baptist Campus Ministries and other college offices.

The best-known version of the haunting is found in Nancy Roberts's book *South Carolina Ghosts: From the Coast to the Mountains*, which incorporates the 1982 article from the *Anderson Independent-Mail*. Roberts describes a male student's encounter in the then Sullivan Music Center with a gently glowing, semi-transparent figure of a young lady seated at a piano. She identifies herself as Anna and as the daughter of the college president. The young man has the presence of mind to quiz the ghost further as to why she remains and how he can help her find peace. The ghost needs his (or someone's) help in encouraging her parents to accept her fiancé, despite their feeling that she is too young to marry and their disapproval of his being Catholic. The interview ends with a threat from the young woman to misbehave unless the man helps her in her quest. The fact that everyone involved is more than likely deceased, not to mention the fact that the entire conversation occurs via telepathy, does not seem to throw the young man off in the least. The next day, the student and his roommate encountered two maintenance men fleeing the Sullivan Center in a high state of distress. The men claimed to have heard a woman singing and playing a piano after hours, in a locked and (supposedly) empty room. Inside Sullivan, the two students encountered a third janitor who described hearing footsteps and finding faucets running in a deserted building. According to Roberts, one of the students claimed that his father was the rejected suitor. In the end, the college provided an official denial that anything tragic has ever happened either on campus or in the music building.

Some other accounts, including one told by an Anderson College alumnus on one website, points out that the Sullivan Building was the college president's house up to the 1940s and confirms that his daughter was unlucky in love. This former student also adds the rumor that the daughter had planned to fake her own suicide by hanging herself off the staircase in the foyer of the building, but that the attempted trick failed. This version also adds that the ghost has been sighted on the lawn in front of the building as well.

The version found in the November 19, 1987 issue of *Echoes*, the Anderson College newsletter, gives no background, just that a girl plays the piano softly and that the lights have been known to go on and off, despite the building being empty.

Of course, I had to try to verify the existence of this lovely phantom. I called Brenda Dubose, a reference librarian at the Olin D. Johnston Memorial Library at Anderson College, and asked her if the Sullivan Building was haunted and if the ghost was still active. She told me that there have been some stories over the years, but that she had not seen or heard anything and that, to her knowledge, there were no ghosts on campus. I asked if that was still the college's official opinion and she said yes.

So, sadly, I could not verify the existence of the lonely lady waiting for her father's blessing, but I have a hunch that on quiet nights, beautifully melancholy music rises from an old piano tucked away in the Sullivan Building followed by the flicker of lights in an empty office.

The old man at a cemetery in Iva

According to a listing of haunted sites in South Carolina, a cemetery in Iva is haunted by an old man who walks behind you until you glance over your shoulder, at which point he vanishes. Legend says that he only appears if you are passing by on foot at sundown. According to the town clerk there are two cemeteries in the town limits of Iva and that office has no information on any ghosts at either of them. The list of sites does not tell which of the two the man haunts or why.

CHEROKEE COUNTY

Cherokee County is located in the north central part of South Carolina. It is bordered by the state of North Carolina, and York, Union and Spartanburg Counties. Native American settlement of the area that is now Cherokee County began about 1000 BC. The area was first settled by whites around 1750, and the county was named for the Cherokee tribe as a result of the long-lasting Native American presence in the area, prior to the 1777 treaty in which they relinquished their land. The area was a hotbed of activity during the Revolution, but only two battles were fought in the present-day county. However, one of these battles—Cowpens—proved that American militia and regulars could defeat British regulars. This defeat also hastened Cornwallis's departure for the supposedly friendlier area of North Carolina, and his eventual surrender at Yorktown, Virginia.

Both before and after the Revolution, modern Cherokee County was a center of iron mining. Many old furnaces and ore pits still remain, hidden in forests. The current area of Cherokee County sent many men to the Confederate army, though no battles were fought there. Cherokee County was formed in 1897 from parts of western Spartanburg, northern Union and eastern York Counties. South Carolina Governor Richard Jeffries was born in present-day Cherokee County, as was actress Andie MacDowell.

"Booger Jim's" bridge

"Booger Jim" haunts the bridge on US Highway 29 over the Broad River, between Gaffney and Blacksburg, near Cherokee Falls. Legend tells that Jim was a local drunk who slept off his binges under the bridge, staying with his wife Becca when he was sober. At some point in 1979, Becca had had it with Jim's drinking and hung him off the side of the bridge with a set of jumper cables. If you call his name on the bridge three times, he will attempt to answer you, but it is very hard to make out his response due to the fact that his vocal cords were crushed when he was hung.

A word to the wise about trying to summon Booger Jim, however: the bridge sees a large amount of tractor-trailer traffic and is very narrow. The shoulders are steep, narrow and soft on both sides of the road. I would park at the intersection of SC Highway 329 and US Highway 29 and walk the quarter mile or so to the bridge. I would recommend a flashlight too, since it gets very dark on the bridge.

I must confess that I came up empty in both the Spartanburg and Gaffney papers for 1979. No bodies were found hanging off the bridge; at least, if one was, it didn't make the papers. But despite the lack of verification from the media, I pushed ahead with my investigation of this tale. I made my first visit to the bridge in mid-March 2005. I arrived at the bridge about four o'clock on a cloudy afternoon to take a few pictures and decided to return at dusk and try to call up the resident ghost.

I returned with a friend around eight o'clock. I wanted actual proof—telepathic whispers or cold spots would probably be written off. After a seemingly lengthy wait for a lull in the traffic, we caught a break of about five minutes and we ran out to the center of the bridge. We stopped and chanted "Booger Jim!" three times in unison. Immediately after the third time, the underbrush on the left-hand side of the highway (facing Blacksburg) began to rustle and a figure appeared before us. Well, *figure* might be too strong a word; a person-sized shadow appeared before us.

As I stared in shock, I felt my friend Michael shove me toward the car. "Semi, coming quick," he whispered, before sprinting back to the car. I jogged back, clearing the bridge before the truck got to the bottom of the hill, and glanced back to see the black shape vanish before the speeding truck's headlights. I then unlocked the car, cranked it up, and we started homeward.

We two gallant fellows were rather pleased with our luck in summoning this specter—until we remembered that the camera had been in the car for safekeeping. Booger Jim would hold his secrets for another evening.

The Gaffney Strangler's ghostly legacy

Leroy Martin, better known as the Gaffney Strangler, may be one of the few forgotten serial killers in American history. Between 1967 and 1968, Martin raped, strangled and left four young women's bodies scattered between Union and Gaffney, South Carolina. Amazingly, one of his victim's husbands was convicted of her murder and was serving a seventeen-year sentence for the crime when Martin confessed. His killing spree started in May 1967 with the rape and strangulation of Annie Desmond, whose body was found off Jerusalem Road in Union County. Two other victims were found on February 8, 1968, followed by the discovery of the final victim eight days later. Martin could likely have gotten away with his crimes, but for the fact that he anonymously called *Gaffney Ledger* editor Bill Gibbons on the day his second two victims were found. Martin was upset that Annie Desmond's husband had been convicted of her murder and wanted him released. He also told Gibbons where to find two additional victims. Nancy Rhinehart's body was found in a brush pile off Chain Gang Road near the Broad River. Nancy Parris was also found that day, along with her dog, under a bridge on Ford Road off SC Highway 329. Martin's calls briefly put Gibbons under suspicion for the murders.

On February 13, 1968, Opal Buckson was kidnapped and later found under some brush in a ditch next to a side road off SC Highway 11. The Gaffney Strangler was arrested on the sixteenth at work at a local textile mill. Martin was convicted after two trials and given four consecutive life sentences. Thankfully, after Martin's repeated statements that he would resume his life of crime if he were ever paroled, a fellow inmate stabbed him to death in his cell on May 31, 1972. At least one of his victims still protests her cruel fate. A poor soul can sometimes be heard screaming and moaning in the night at the bridge over an unnamed creek on Ford Road off SC 329. This first bridge off SC 329 on Ford Road (going south toward Wilkinsville and Union) is where the body of Nancy Parris and that of her dog were found in February 1968. If you walk across the bridge at night, you can hear her moans of pain and cries for help.

Following my success summoning Booger Jim, I was inspired to try my luck on Nancy's bridge. I stopped in the middle of the bridge and cut the car off for a second or two, hoping that I would still hear her cries and offer her some kind words and encourage her to find peace. I noticed that the bridge I was sitting on was a replacement for the original one; it was dated 2000 on its side. My wife refused to get out of the car, so I agreed to stop only for a moment. I was not as lucky with our compromise, however. I still believe that if I had gotten out of the car and walked the bridge, despite my wife's protests I would have had an experience. No cries broke the silence of the night, just some tree frogs and the murmur of the creek below. After about a minute or so, I said a brief prayer for Nancy Parris and continued home.

Limestone College:
More than just Gaylord Perry

The reason for this section heading is simple: the only thing most folks from outside the Upstate know about Limestone College in Gaffney, if they have ever heard of it at all, is that two-time Cy Young Award winner and baseball Hall of Famer Gaylord Perry was once the baseball coach there. In fact, Perry started the baseball program at Limestone. Limestone College was founded by Dr. Charles Curtis in 1845 and is now a private four-year college. Half the buildings on campus are on the National Register of Historic Places, including the chapel.

The chapel at Limestone College resembles a small-town Baptist church, complete with steeple. Not exactly a sight to conjure up ghosts; but over the years I have learned that most ghosts avoid their stereotypical haunts. The legend behind the haunting has a basis in that oldest of human emotions—anger. Two girls were playing on the stairs leading up to the balcony one afternoon. (I would supply an approximate date, but no record of these events has been found concerning the chapel, so I would not want to speculate.) Over the course of the afternoon, one of the girls got mad at the other and pushed her friend down the stairs. The poor child broke her neck and died due to the fall. Since then, in the late afternoon, custodians and others who have been in the chapel have claimed to have seen a blue shape quickly appear and disappear on the balcony stairs, sometimes accompanied by a child's laughter. The young girl who died was wearing a blue dress.

Another story I came across concerning Limestone's campus focused on a nearby apartment complex used primarily by students. One of the renters found her hot water being cut on every night at 3:00 a.m. Though the plumbing was investigated and even replaced, the mysterious occurrence continued. Finally, the young woman made a verbal request to the uninvited guest to only use the water when she was not home. Only this brought her any peace.

During my investigation of the haunts at Limestone College, I unfortunately did not have the pleasure to see anything firsthand. The same day I took photos at Booger Jim's bridge, I got an exterior photo of the chapel, hoping to catch the young girl's ghost at play. Nothing appeared on the shot and I did not hear anything unusual. The next Monday, I called Dr. Craig Kubias, the college chaplain, to see if he had had or heard of any unusual experiences in the chapel. He told me that he had heard the stories but had never seen or heard anything himself. He also referred me to the college president's office to see if anyone had reported anything unusual. The person I spoke to, whose name I have misplaced under a stack of research, told me in no uncertain terms that the campus was not haunted and that I was wasting my time. However, I feel that there have been too many reports of the sightings and hauntings, and that these reports are too similar, to be a hoax or the products of an overactive imagination.

As mythical as the unicorn…and as hard to find

The four stories that follow have nothing in common except their location in Cherokee County. Three of these are apparently just "spook stories," but they still haunt the memories of the witnesses and their listeners.

The story at Blacksburg Middle School is the most credible of the four. According to legend, a female basketball player hung herself in the school gymnasium following a win in 1980. Her ghost has supposedly been seen in the school building and the lights in the gym have been known to go on and off at odd hours. Sadly, I could not find any evidence of a Blacksburg Middle School student dying suddenly in 1980 in any of the area newspapers. The school denied that any student had committed suicide on school grounds. During my ghost photo tour of the Gaffney area, my friends and I rode past the middle school after dark but found the gym, like the rest of the school, to be dark and empty.

Another local legend is Rock House Road. The rock house, which supposedly can only be seen once a year (though my sources conflicted on the dates it is visible), is said to be haunted by a little girl who was mentally impaired. She went out after dark with a candle, got lost when it blew out, and died from exposure. As the story goes, if you hold a candle up to a window at the house, her face will appear. I did locate the road after leaving Kings Mountain National Military Park, but I saw no rock house on the whole length of it.

Another haunted road in Cherokee County is said to be Carson Drive. According to legend, a white dog has been appearing to (and disappearing from) people walking and driving by on this residential street near the Draytonville community for the last ten years or so. The dog is not blamed for any accidents or injuries, but it does have one unusual attribute: he has been known to walk on two legs and run toward witnesses. I drove Carson Drive alone one Saturday night, but never saw anything unusual, and no dog ran after me on its back legs.

Blast Battleground and Cemetery are apparently the same location under different names and is located somewhere near Crestview Church on SC Highway 11, near Daniel Morgan Elementary School. In this rural family cemetery, it is said one can hear the sounds of cannon fire and gunshots. If you step away and return, you will then see men fighting with small arms and swords. These people will respond if you move or speak by making death threats against you. This lurid tale continues with the warning that some visitors to the cemetery have been injured and some have even disappeared! I of course had to find this cemetery and see for myself these early battlers. I must have driven more than fifty miles on back roads, looking for likely spots within a mile of Crestview Church. There are a handful of graves on the church's lot but nothing as organized as a formal church cemetery. I had planned to go stand in the cemetery after dark and take turns walking in and out until the phenomenon really got active. Unfortunately, though, after more than a dozen sudden stops and about an hour of wandering around in the woods at twilight, I still hadn't found the cemetery. I even stopped at a nearby gas station and asked about the Blast Cemetery. The cashier directed me to the large, perpetual-care cemetery about a mile back toward Gaffney and said that it was the only big cemetery anywhere nearby. It would have been fun to have witnessed the outbreak of a battle of ghosts, who apparently take offense at the presence of living witnesses; I'll have to continue my search another day.

CHESTER COUNTY

Chester County is in the north central part of South Carolina. It is bordered by York, Union, Lancaster and Fairfield Counties. The area now included in the county was a common and popular hunting ground for both the Cherokee and Catawba Indian tribes prior to the start of white settlement around 1750. The majority of these early settlers were Ulster Scots and Scotch-Irish Covenanter Presbyterians and many descendants of the original settlers have remained in the area.

Chester County witnessed some early anti-British agitation prior to the Revolution and supplied many men and supplies to both sides during that conflict. Present-day Chester County was the scene of four battles during the Revolution. General Sherman passed through the southeastern corner of the county en route to Chesterfield and North Carolina from Columbia. The Confederate Constitution, along with other records and documents, were saved from looters at the former Southern Railway depot in downtown Chester in March 1865. The county was named for the city of Chester in Pennsylvania, which was in turn named for the city in England. Since a large numbers of the early settlers came down the Appalachians and were from the west of England originally, this is a logical progression.

Chester County was one of the first counties formed in South Carolina, dating its existence to the 1785 state constitution. No state governors or U.S. senators have come from Chester, but Marty Marion, 1944 National

League MVP, and Jayel Wylie, noted romance author, were both born here. William Richardson Davie, "Father of the University of North Carolina," was also born in Chester County. Chester County is also known for the films that have been made, either in whole or in part, in the county. These include *Chiefs*, a miniseries starring Charlton Heston, and *The Patriot*, starring Mel Gibson.

Bethel United Methodist Church

This particular tale of my adopted county is odd in that I learned of it from a ten-year-old girl. But first, some historical background is in order. Bethel United Methodist Church was founded in 1837 and moved to its present location in 1897. Bethel was the first Methodist church established in the city limits of Chester.

The story of the lady in the nursery has been told by generations of Sunday schoolers at Bethel. According to my original source, Stavia Stone-Wylder, she and a friend were playing upstairs one Sunday after church near the nursery when they passed a locked room. From the hallway they both heard the sound of a piano. After listening for moment, the two girls realized that the light in the room was off and that the door was locked from the hall side. When the two girls told Stavia's mother what they had heard, they discovered that the room had been a piano room about thirty years ago, but was now only used for storage.

Upon hearing this rather unexpected tale, I called the church office and spoke to the secretary, Jane Carter. She has worked at Bethel for almost twenty years and has heard footsteps in that hall at all hours since her first day, but has not heard the piano playing at odd hours. According to her account, the pastor at Bethel has seen a woman in a 1970s-style pantsuit inside the nursery. Ms. Carter says that he has seen the woman through the large window from his office across the hall, just looking around. According to Mrs. Carter, the pastor has also felt a breeze he thought might be caused by the ghost passing him in the hall, even though the hall appears to be empty. He has also complained of cold spots in his office and in the nursery. Of course, the truly curious thing is that no one knows who this woman is and no one has ever died in the building. Speculation is that she is a nursery volunteer who died at home, but who still feels an obligation to check on her old church and charges. The pastor at Bethel United Methodist Church declined to be interviewed for this book about his experiences.

Dan Bell, the Chester ARP Church and the Chester Little Theater

This story is the reason I wanted to write this book. So many different sites have been touched by Dan Bell's death in my adopted hometown and none of the published sources have even mentioned these hauntings at all. At most, the accounts say that the Chester Little Theater is the site of many strange and unusual things including unexplained noises and apparitions. The hauntings at the Chester Associate Presbyterian (ARP) Church, Chester Little Theater and the former site of Barron's Funeral Home occur along most of one side of Wylie Street in downtown Chester. There is so much more to this story, as you will soon see.

According to some older citizens of Chester, the area where the Little Theater is now was the site of the public gallows as far back as the 1780s. However, the gallows have also been reputedly located on Henry Woods Drive and at the first old jail, now a law office. The more likely explanation for the haunting of the Chester Little Theater dates from the early 1930s. In July 1932, the Bell family owned and operated the Chester Telephone Company. These Bells were not related by blood to Alexander Graham Bell; the common name is just a happy accident of history. The long-distance operators for the phone company were located at 109 Wylie Street, now the Chester ARP Church offices. Next door to them was Barron's Funeral Home, at 105 Wylie, then the City (now known as the Powell) Theater at 103 Wylie. The operators were on the second floor of the telephone company building.

On July 14, 1932, young Daniel Bell was preparing to take a bath and struck a match to light a lamp in a basement on Wylie Street. Apparently, the shower was provided for employees to clean up if they got dirty during the workday. The *Chester Reporter* newspaper account dated July 18, 1932, states that Mr. Bell was in the telephone company basement when he struck this fatal match, setting alight some escaping gas and causing the boiler to explode. Despite being severely burned and nude, Mr. Bell gave no thought to his own welfare, but darted upstairs to warn the female operators of the danger, getting the three that were on duty out of the building with only minor injuries. Mr. Bell died of his wounds on Saturday the sixteenth of July 1932.

However, the most commonly told version of the story places Mr. Bell and his bath next door in the basement of Barron's Funeral Home. His personal bravery can not be discounted, though, as regardless of where he was bathing, he did save the lives of the three ladies at work for his family's firm. The boiler explosion was blamed on a faulty pilot light and phone service was quickly reconnected.

Barron's Funeral Home left the 105 Wylie Street location by 1940 and moved to 133 Wylie Street, about a block away. Chester Telephone stayed at the Wylie Street location until 1953, when it relocated to offices on York Street. However, Dan Bell is still very much a part of life on Wylie Street, even more than seventy years after his death.

Odd events have occurred at the Chester ARP Church offices in the old Bell Annex at 109 Wylie Street since the church acquired it in 1981. Linda Tinker, church secretary, told me that she has heard male voices and footsteps upstairs at odd hours and that once a former pastor told her to stop talking so loud, as he was on the phone. She was outside smoking at the time. She has also heard footsteps on the steps leading to the second floor as well.

When I went to examine the area, I heard no one upstairs but I did feel a breeze while looking around, as if I had been passed by someone in a hurry. Also, off the pastor's office is a short (two-step) staircase leading to a small area. There is an old boiler and a concrete floor here, along with some odds and ends in storage. I saw nothing while I was down there, but as I was shutting the door I heard heavy footsteps walk across the dirty concrete. Mrs. Tinker has also heard her name called while she sat in an otherwise empty office. Ms. Chris Clayton, the church custodian, told me that she has heard footsteps and a male voice in the vacant sanctuary while she was at work.

Moving down the block, 105 Wylie Street is for rent and is currently empty, having seen several tenants come and go over the years. However, you can gain access to the rear of the building through the second floor of the Chester Little Theater building. Traces of the site's past as a funeral home are still there, though. At the rear of the site, a room once used for embalming corpses still stands ready for use. Tools lie on a counter and an uncovered drain is visible in the center of the floor. Next door, behind the ARP Church's garage, the dumbwaiter used to lift the bodies from the ambulance or hearse still stands; its hand-carved wooden gears still intact. Over the garage itself, the coffin storage area is still there, the wooden doors pulled down.

Along the hall running from the dumbwaiter to the stairs to the lobby below, people working on sets and running lines in the auditorium of the theater next door claim to have heard the squeak of a gurney's wheels on a tile floor. No apparitions have yet appeared, but the squeak of a phantom gurney will send chills up your spine.

Despite the activity at the other two sites on Wylie Street, the real hot spot is the old Powell Theater building at 103 Wylie Street, now home to the Chester Little Theater. More than six different ghosts have made their presences felt in the building over the years. The most recent haunt to appear is the ghost of a woman found stuffed into a dumpster in the alley at the rear of the backstage area in the early 1980s. Terry Cameron was inside the building sewing costumes when she heard a thump on the wall behind her. Looking out into the alley, she saw no one and returned to work. The next morning, the body was found and no one has yet identified the body. Naturally, Terry does not volunteer to work in the building alone now. Several years after the murder, a bathroom for actors and others backstage was built just inside the building from where the body was found. This bathroom has since been notorious for cold spots and for faucets inexplicably turning on and off. There have been bangs and thumps heard on the outside wall as well. When the area is checked, no evidence is ever found of any recent human activity.

The stage at the Little Theater is also a hot spot for activity. Facing the stage, the area in the wings on the front right is known as "Norm's spot." Norm was a prop handler who always stood in the same spot on stage. After his suicide, which *did not* happen at the theater, the odd happenings in the area began. Actors have been known to trip here for no reason; props have constantly been misplaced; and cold spots have been reported. As annoying as these can be, they are nothing compared to the shock that Terry Cameron and Becky White got one night after a rehearsal. They were going up the aisle when a flicker from the stage caught their eyes. Having no idea where the light came from, they turned and saw two cylinders of light on the stage moving back and forth. After calmly watching for about a minute, both ladies felt goose bumps and hurriedly left the building. The former projection booth was not yet enclosed at the time of this incident, but the movement of the cylinders seems to eliminate any reflection as the source.

To end our tour of the stage area, let's look at two cases of auditory manifestation. Both cases happened during rehearsals, one during *Man of La Mancha*. The cast was using a tape recording to fix the words of the songs in their minds. The psalm was the focal point of the night's activity. Up to that point, all had gone as expected. But when Glinda Price Coleman cued up that particular song (after the tape had been left onstage overnight), it played back in reverse. No other songs were the least bit out of the ordinary. After rehearsal, Mrs. Price Coleman played the tape in her car while going home, and the playback was normal on every track, even the psalm.

The second odd auditory event happened during a dress rehearsal for *All Because of Agatha*. The stage manager, Mrs. Alice Addison, was using a headset to communicate from backstage to the lighting booth. Halfway through act 1, Mrs. Addison came on stage as white as a ghost and shaking. She insisted that everyone listen to her headset. Those present heard a baby crying at the top of its lungs. There was not a baby present at the time and when the headset was cut off, no crying was heard. Everyone laughed it off as merely interference from a nearby baby monitor until the group realized that the nearest house was about a quarter of a mile away.

Voices, footsteps, creaks and other noises have disturbed many rehearsals. But the stage area is not the only part of the theater where odd events have occurred. Both the stage and the seating areas have attracted large numbers of visible orbs. Orbs are typically visible only in photographs, but are usually accompanied by cold spots or other physical manifestations. During my visits to the theater in the last year, I have taken many photographs—some in which orbs are present. Since the Chester Little Theater (and the whole side of Wylie Street, for that matter) is seemingly infested with orbs, let me address these problematic manifestations here. Most photographs of many stationary orbs are, in all likelihood, simply dust particles reflecting the light from a camera's flash. Photographs with movement or color change, or single, well-defined orbs, are more likely to be manifestations of a ghost of some kind.

In one photograph I took, an orb was present; in my second shot less than five seconds later, the orb was gone. At the time of my first photo, Al Pratt, a veteran actor and middle school history teacher who was there with me during this particular hunt, was describing the presence of an older white woman just outside his reach. Shortly after the second photo was taken, Mr. Pratt reported that the lady was gone. With your back to the stage, the area where he saw the image is in the rear of the seating area on your left.

Upstairs in the set storage area curious things have appeared in the windows facing Wylie Street. Nikki Bramlett, a longtime actor and director at the theater, saw a white woman in her sixties staring down at the street from the window. One photograph I took of the exterior of the building showed an orb in this window. This occurred in February of 2005 during rehearsals for the show *Five Women Wearing the Same Dress*. This figure, sighted by Ms. Bramlett and possibly caught by my camera, may be the same woman who beckoned to me from the top of the lobby stairs while I was waiting for the intermission of *My Three Angels*. Sadly, I have no idea what she wanted, as discretion overcame my usual impulsiveness and I declined her invitation. Shortly after her appearance, one of the stagehands came up and drafted me into filling in for a sick actor. He did not see the lady or notice how pale I was. Her identity remains unknown; I have no information on any older woman coming to any sort of harm on the site.

Another area in the old Powell Theater to hold a haunt is the former balcony, now used for prop storage and lighting. According to unverified local lore, a young black female was raped on the stairs leading from the alley up to the balcony. During the assault, she hit her head on the concrete floor and later died en route to the hospital. Her presence has reportedly been felt many times on the narrow stairs. Cold spots and a sensation of being short of breath have struck many people while climbing the stairs in the area, including myself during a ghost hunt at the theater in October 2004. On this same hunt, I heard the distinctive slapping sound of a film running off its reel while I was looking around in the deserted old projection booth. A slightly more terrifying attack happened to my sister-in-law, Jessica. She was coming down the narrow stairs from the top rack of lights to the balcony when she was pushed from behind by an invisible set of hands. Thankfully, she caught herself before falling over the railing to the floor below.

During a hunt a few years before, Johnny Roddey, a longtime actor and board member at the theater had a scare of his own when he disturbed a flock of pigeons in the projection booth, causing him and the five people with him to run screaming into the street below.

The Wylie Street area of historic downtown Chester has many ghosts, but by no means holds a monopoly on the county's haunts. As you will soon discover, Great Falls, the second city of the county, has a few ghosts of its own.

Great Falls: The Red Room

Great Falls is located in the extreme southeastern corner of Chester County. It was one of three sites chosen for United States arsenals by Secretary of War Henry Dearborn in 1803. As such, it was on the list of contenders for the site of the US Military Academy, along with Harpers Ferry, Virginia, and West Point, New York. The ruins of Mount Dearborn can still be seen on an island in the Catawba River. Great Falls began life as a textile mill town with a background in hydropower. In 1904 Dr. W. Gill Wylie, James B. Duke and W. States Lee decided to build a hydropower plant at the Great Falls of the Catawba. From this small beginning sprang the regional power colossus better known as Duke Energy.

The Memorial Building in Great Falls honors all veterans, especially those of World War II. It is a two-story house and is the site of the Flopeye Festival, held every year on Memorial Day weekend. The Memorial Building is used as meeting space for many civil and community groups, including the local Boy Scout troop. One of the groups headquartered in the building is the Great Falls Home Town Association, headed by Mrs. Glinda Price Coleman. Mrs. Price Coleman has led the association since 2001 and has not had any odd experiences in the building. However, she has heard the legend.

Shortly after the building's construction in the early 1920s, and well before it became the Memorial Building in the early 1950s, the house was home to a childless couple. As is so often the case, the names of the unfortunate couple have been lost over the years. The marriage was apparently not a happy one, as the wife was having an affair. As the story goes, the husband came home from work at one of the textile mills in town to find his wife in her lover's embrace. The husband was in such a fury that he grabbed a handy axe and hacked them both to death in the bedroom. The blood and gore splattered the walls and floor of the room. The husband seems to have vanished from history immediately following this crime of passion—perhaps he fell victim to the currents of the Catawba in remorse. In any event, the crime scene was soon discovered and cleaned up. New paint was put on the walls and the house was offered for sale. After going through a rapid succession of owners, the house was offered to the town. The reason given for the quick turnover of tenants was the bloodstains in the upstairs bedroom. According to witnesses, the stains simply reappeared through all colors of paints, regardless of the thickness of coats. For this reason, the scene of the crime acquired the nickname of the "Red Room."

Mrs. Price Coleman told me that all of the rooms upstairs now have wallpaper and that no stains are visible, but admitted that some locals who drop in will not go upstairs for any reason. All she herself has heard is some scratching inside the walls, but she is more inclined to blame squirrels than ghosts. She also said that the Boy Scouts meet upstairs and have reported no problems.

My only visit to the Great Falls Memorial Building came during the Flopeye Festival in 1998. I was there doing publicity for a local political campaign. After an interview with a local radio station, I entered the building to use the restroom. On my way out, I heard footsteps upstairs. Since I had seen no one else enter with me, my curiosity was aroused. I went upstairs, thinking that perhaps someone had gotten lost looking for the restroom or otherwise needed a hand. No one else was upstairs. In fact, as I was coming downstairs I was told in no uncertain terms that the upstairs area was closed to the public. Sadly, I didn't think to peek into any of the rooms to check for bloodstains, but maybe on my next trip I will visit the Red Room.

The hitchhiker of Nitrolee Dam

Until I went to Great Falls Middle School and did a storytelling appearance, I thought that the Red Room was the only haunted site in the area. When I asked the class to write their own "true" ghost stories, one place kept reappearing: the bridge below the Nitrolee Dam. The bridge is located over the Catawba River just below the dam. On the Chester County side of the river, US Highway 21 and SC Highways 97 and 200 merge just before the bridge, while on the Lancaster County side, SC Highways 97 and 200 split just after crossing the River. With all these major traffic arteries separating and then coming together, and the high volume of traffic during the years when all three textile mills were running in Great Falls, serious accidents were not uncommon. This bridge has seen a fair number of fatal crashes over the years and the haunting dates back to the 1950s, according to the accounts I have come across.

According to the legend, at some point during the 1950s, a young woman was driving home from her second shift at the Republic #2 Mill in Great Falls at about midnight when her car crossed the center line and was hit head-on by a logging truck. The impact knocked the car over the guardrail and into the riverbed between the dam and bridge. The woman's mangled body was found in the wreckage. Rainy, foggy weather was blamed, along with the woman's exhaustion. A horrible thing, but not that unusual, right?

Not until the woman started flagging down trucks that were speeding across the bridge. Well, flagging down might be an understatement—in fact she was running out in front of them on a narrow, two-lane bridge in the rain. All the truckers who have seen her over the years say that she was not there and then she was, dashing across the bridge as soon as their headlights hit it. Rumor has it that she still appears, as a warning to truckers to slow down and to be more careful. I have driven through the area and over the bridge after dark on several occasions and never seen anything. Apparently only truckers can see her, but perhaps you will have a bit more luck.

Yet more cry baby bridges

Chester County is unusual in that there are two different "cry baby bridges" in the area. The first one is in the northern part of the county, near the York County line on Mills Road. Rumor has it that a woman threw her baby off the bridge into the shallow branch below in order to spite her cheating husband. None of my sources have been able to determine when this heinous act occurred or who the depraved woman was. The odd thing about the tale of this haunting is that the baby's cries are said to be heard without any ritual being performed. Just drive over the bridge and you'll hear the cries of an infant from the waters below. I have driven to and stopped on this bridge and the effect is uncanny. As soon as the car stops moving, the quiet country air is split by the cries of a baby in pain.

The second cry baby bridge of Chester County is rumored to be located on Ashford Road in the central part of the county, south of the city of Chester. Here the traditional ritual still applies. You must stop your car in the center of the bridge, blow you horn, and a baby's cries will arise from the creek below. Unfortunately, the legend does not specify *which* bridge on Ashford Road is the home of this phantom baby—there are three different bridges over creeks on Ashford Road. I have tried to verify the story, but have had no results on any of the bridges.

Gene's Restaurant: Footsteps with your meal?

I am a creature of habit. I eat breakfast and lunch at the same place every weekday I am in town. It's a cafeteria-style diner named Gene's Restaurant on

Gadsden Street in downtown Chester. It may not have the greatest atmosphere, but the coffee is great, the waitresses are cute, and you can still smoke inside.

The restaurant occupies the ground floor and the second floor is vacant. Imagine my shock and that of some of my fellow coffee lovers when we heard footsteps overhead about eight o'clock one morning in January 2005. We were all amazed and asked Bill Robertson, the owner and chef of Gene's, what was going on. He merely said it was the old man who used to live upstairs when it was an apartment— the man in question died shortly after Bill bought the place. I've never heard it again, but I keep waiting.

The Ridgeview Road light

Ridgeview Road is a typical Southern back road. A few small houses, a handful of mobile homes and lots and lots of timberland line the narrow strip of asphalt. It is a dead-end street and a perfect hideout for whitetail deer. In fact, most of the open land along the road is leased to hunt clubs.

After dark, an unusual event occurs on an old, unnamed gated logging road leading into the woods off Ridgeview Road. According to the legend, the road was originally a driveway to a house. A child died there, some say in his sleep, others say he was killed in a tragic accident with a mechanical hay bailer. A sad story, but not that unusual in the rural South a few decades back. What makes this case unusual is that the spirit of the child still appears on the old road. To summon the ghost, you need to drive to the gate at night and blow your horn. A ball of white light will appear, dancing between the trees and hovering in the night sky.

I attempted to summon the light by following the ritual but had no luck. I can only guess that you need to get further past the locked gate for it to work, but since that would be trespassing and it was hunting season, discretion and caution defeated my curiosity that night.

A Chester collection of ghostlore

The following hauntings have all occurred in private homes and have either happened to me personally, as in the first two cases, or have received attention in published sources. My wife's family lives on Henry Woods Drive in Chester. Henry Woods Drive is one of two sites mentioned as a candidate for the first set of gallows within the city limits. (The other is the parking lot on Wylie Street across from the Powell Theater, now home to the Chester Little Theater as described above.) The Henry Woods area is a quiet residential neighborhood located behind the Chester County School District office. But in a 1982 article for the journal *Names in South Carolina*, John Bigham described the area as "one to be avoided." Indeed, my wife Rachel and I witnessed some odd events at her parents' house while we were dating. We had been dating for about two years when Rachel's cat, named Rooster, died. Rooster had been fond of walking from the oven to the dryer by way of the countertop, despite the fact that this was forbidden territory. The weekend after Rooster's death, Rachel and I were watching TV late Saturday night when movement in the kitchen caught our eyes. We both shouted, "Get down, Rooster!" before realizing that he was no longer the guilty party. The next morning, when we mentioned our sighting to Rachel's mother, she merely said, "Just tell him to get down and he will, just like always. He just misses us. I've seen him a lot."

The other haunting that I witnessed in a private residence was in my own apartment in a thirty-year-old duplex on the west side of Chester. It was the only time I have seen a ghost there. It was the night before my wedding to Rachel. I was in bed reading and smoking. About eleven o'clock, I glanced up and saw a man standing in front of my refrigerator. The man turned toward me, smiled, nodded and walked toward the front door. After a few seconds, I jumped up, checked both the locked sliding glass back door and the dead-bolted front door, and then stopped in my tracks. It dawned on me that I had recognized the man. It was my great-grandfather, who had died of cancer about seven years before. Great-grandfather, or "Papa" as I had called him, had practically raised me, and I was devoted to him. I had expressed regret just a few days before that he would miss my wedding. I really think he came back to reassure me that everything would be fine and that he wasn't going to miss anything. My best friend, Bill Roddey, and his girlfriend, Susan Hoff, say that they've heard people stomping around our apartment when we are out. Sadly, I haven't heard them myself, but I would hope that I'm lucky enough to live in a haunted apartment.

The final private residence in Chester County that is documented to be haunted is the Lowry-Erwin House, located in the community of Lowrys in northern Chester County. The house and the odd events that have occurred there were written about in both *South Carolina: A Guide to the Palmetto State* and *Palmetto Place Names*, both published by the WPA in the 1940s. The Lowry-

Erwin House was built in 1800 by Parson J.G. Lowry, a Presbyterian minister and revivalist. According to local legend, Parson Lowry still haunts his old home. According to local lore, he hid his life's savings in gaps in the walls and returns to ensure that the money remains undiscovered. Strange noises in the attic and footsteps on the stairs are blamed on the parson's ghost. I have not found any more recent accounts than those the WPA collected, but the house still stands and is a local landmark.

FAIRFIELD COUNTY

Fairfield County is located in the northern part of the state. It is bordered by Chester, Lancaster, Kershaw, Richland, Newberry and Union Counties. Native Americans, like the Catawba tribe, used the area mainly as a hunting ground, but burial mounds and other traces of settlement have been found here and dated back to roughly 1500 BC. White settlement began about 1750. Fairfield County was named by the British General Cornwallis while he was camped in the Winnsboro area during the Revolution. He reportedly exclaimed, "What Fair Fields!" and the name stuck. Three Revolutionary battles were fought in the area. During the Civil War, part of Winnsboro, the county seat, was burned by Sherman's troops on their way north toward Bentonsville following the burning of Columbia. Fairfield County was the birthplace of one governor of South Carolina, John H. Means. Parr Shoals, on the Broad River, was the site of the first atomic power plant built in the southeastern United States, in 1962.

Downtown Winnsboro

The Fairfield Museum is located in historic downtown Winnsboro. The building was built in 1832 as a private residence. Up until the Civil War, it served as a girls' school ran by Catherine Ladd. During the Union occupation of the town, the house served as an officers' barracks, then reverted back to use as a private residence. In the late 1990s, Ms. Pelham Lyles, the researcher at the Fairfield Museum, was told by a self-described psychic that she had sensed two men in uniform fighting on the third-floor stairs. Ms. Lyles herself has had some odd experiences while alone in the building. She has heard footsteps and bumps on the third floor, as well as seeing extension cords moving on the floor without visible reason. The cleaning person will not go into the building alone after dark, but will not explain why. Once, on a Halloween ghost tour sponsored by several civic groups, the tour guide's candle went all the way out, and then flickered back to life while on the third floor. A member of the tour said that they had seen an old lady sitting at a table in the research room and asked who the actress was. The guide explained that there was no one acting out any stories on the tour.

The museum is not the only haunted site on South Congress Street. Its next-door neighbor, the old Beaty House, is now the home of the Goode Law Firm. Workers there have heard what sounds like a man's heavy footsteps on a hardwood floor, but the entire building is now carpeted. The footsteps seem to walk up to the conference room door, but when the door is opened no one is in the hall. Items have been knocked or thrown off the walls and file cabinet and desk drawers have been found open in the morning after being left locked overnight. No one at the law firm would comment on these reported occurrences. The building once served as a girls' school in antebellum days and was used during the Union occupation of Winnsboro as a hospital. The man is believed to be one of the patients who died there.

The final haunting I have found in Winnsboro is at the Tavern Restaurant. It is located behind the clock tower, which is a prominent landmark downtown. The building staff has reported hearing a woman whispering what may be a man's name, after closing. None of the staff I spoke to had heard the voice themselves, but they all had heard the story. No one knows why the woman whispers, but I suspect unrequited love may have something to do with it.

Does Colonel Provence still walk?

Colonel David Provence was a veteran of the War of 1812 from Kentucky who came to the Monticello section of Fairfield County to marry a Miss Hall in 1836. The legend surrounding his ghost is not very well known outside Fairfield County. I found the outline of the story in *A Fairfield Sketchbook* by J.S. Bolick. Colonel Provence was an eccentric by the standards of his time and loved horse racing and the social whirl. He was buried across the street from Rock Creek Baptist Church, near his home of Rose Hill. There are three different reasons for this, according to legend. The first reason is that he did not wish to be buried with the "common herd," in his words. The second and third reasons concern his Catholic faith. One theory had it that he did not wish to be buried among "heretics," and the other is that the church members did not want him buried with them. Hence, he was laid to rest in a solitary grave on a hilltop across the road.

At the turn of the century, granite quarrying became a major industry in Fairfield County and many Italian stonecutters came into the area. One night, some of these men, having heard rumors that the late colonel tried to take some of his wealth with him to the afterlife, dug up his body and disturbed his remains, leaving his body on the ground next to the grave marker. After this desecration, the colonel's ghost began his wandering. The ghost has been seen both near the cemetery and near the gate to Rose Hill. Speculation has it that the colonel had buried some important papers in the church cemetery, but nothing has yet been found to prove this rumor. The reason given for his coming to the gate of his former home was that he simply wanted to make sure all was well.

However, when the Monticello Reservoir was built, the cemetery for Rock Creek Church was not moved and neither was Colonel Provence's grave. The waters of the Broad River covered all traces of the legend. So we will just have to hope that Colonel Provence found peace before Parr Shoals Dam was finished on Broad River. To my knowledge, no one has reported any sightings or other odd happenings at the dam.

GREENVILLE COUNTY

Greenville County is in the northwestern part of South Carolina. It is bordered by the state of North Carolina and Spartanburg, Laurens, Anderson and Pickens Counties. Greenville County was primarily home to the Cherokee Indian tribe from roughly 1000 BC to the American Revolution. In fact, until the formation of the county in 1786, the area was held as Indian territory after the tribe's defeat in the Cherokee War of 1760–61.

Present-day Greenville County was the site of three battles in the Revolution. The area was also a hotbed of Unionist views from the 1830s until secession in 1860. Exactly where the name "Greenville" came from is a matter of some debate. One theory is that it was named for the Revolutionary hero General Nathanael Greene, though there are no records to indicate he had any ties to the area. The second theory is that it was named for the verdant green countryside encountered by the first white settlers, who began arriving about 1755 or so. The WPA publication *Palmetto Place Names* gives priority to the first theory, while the journal *Names in South Carolina* favors the color theory, pointing out that the area was largely settled by veterans of the Revolution who were not big fans of General Greene, despite mentioning John C. Calhoun's support for the Greene theory. Apparently, General Greene was a stern taskmaster who did not attract the love and devotion of his soldiers. Another supporter of the color theory was Robert Mills, state engineer in the 1820s and designer of the Washington Monument.

Greenville County is home to several institutions of higher learning, including Bob Jones University and Furman University. The city of Greenville is also an industrial center and one of the largest cities in the state. Among well-known people from Greenville County are "Shoeless" Joe Jackson, longtime star for the Chicago White Sox and member of the infamous 1919 "Black Sox"; Jesse Jackson, civil rights leader and two-time presidential candidate; and Dick Riley, former South Carolina governor and the secretary of education under President Clinton. Other governors from Greenville County include Carroll Campbell and Benjamin F. Perry.

Embassy Suites: Room for one more?

The Embassy Suites Hotel in Greenville is a popular destination for visiting executives and other tourists. It is also rumored to be one of the most haunted spots in the county. Interestingly, the person I spoke to at the hotel had heard of no complaints, knew no stories and repeatedly expressed amazement when asked about a possible haunting at the site. Roger Wellington, librarian in the South Carolina Room at the Greenville County Library, could find no reason, such as an abandoned cemetery or sensational crime, to explain why the site might be haunted. However, local legend has it otherwise. According to the tale, the hotel is home to a classic figure in ghost stories—a poltergeist.

Poltergeists (German for "rumbling ghosts") are invisible spirits that interact with the living by way of lights, doors and other inanimate objects. During construction of the Embassy Suites building, lights were reported on in the building, despite the absence of power. The police would check the scene for vagrants and vandals and find no one there at all, nor evidence of any intruders.

The Verdae Greens Golf Course, on which the Embassy Suites is located, has three different areas where grass will not grow, according to local lore. Other incidents on the golf course have included a strange wailing noise and the movement of shrubbery without any apparent cause.

Tanglewood Middle School: A myth with a core of fact

Tanglewood Middle School is located on the east side of Greenville and is reportedly haunted.

The stories date from the school's construction in the 1950s. According to one legend, a student was killed by an unknown assailant in the girls' locker room not long after the school opened. The victim still makes her presence felt by slamming doors and appearing as a dark shadow. In the boys' locker room, the showers are said to go on and off by themselves, and locker doors slam without human help. The lights in both locker rooms are also prone to going off unaided as well.

The sixth-grade hall is another hot spot, according to this tale. On rainy days, you can see wet footprints appear in the hall when you are alone. Supposedly, this hall is also the site of an even more gruesome occurrence. According to local lore, a madman entered the school, killed almost all of the students on the sixth-grade hall and escaped. This horrible crime occurred in the 1950s, according to one account, though I could not locate any accounts of it in the local press. Now the blood from this attack is said to seep through the paint on the current sixth-grade hall, despite repeated attempts to paint over it. The actual scene of the crime was supposedly buried afterward and doorframes and other traces have been uncovered.

Rather than attempt to investigate this account on site and risk disrupting a school day, I decided to contact the media specialist at Tanglewood, Ms. Roberta Nance. I asked if she or any of her colleagues had any information on the school's haunted reputation. Mrs. Melinda Long, an eighth-grade English and language arts teacher, confessed that most of the reported incidents at Tanglewood are fiction, fashioned by a creative teacher who enjoys tormenting young minds, though she did not name this person. Mrs. Long did tell me one true story, however. A few years ago, a cafeteria worker fell ill at work and went to her doctor's office. Upon arrival, the woman died of a heart attack. By all accounts, she was a pleasant, friendly person. After her sudden death, some staffers and custodians claimed to have seen her in and around the cafeteria. The sightings lasted for a few months then gradually stopped, according to Mrs. Long.

Poinsett Bridge

Poinsett Bridge is located in the northern part of Greenville County. It was built with slave labor under the direction of Joel R. Poinsett, first United States minister to Mexico and later secretary of war in the cabinet of President Martin Van Buren. The poinsettia plant is his namesake.

The bridge was built in 1820 as part of the state road designed to link the Upstate and the Lowcountry of South Carolina. Poinsett had the bridge named after him for his leadership of the State Board of Public Works from 1818 to 1820. Today it is closed to automotive traffic, but still open to hikers.

The bridge is haunted by those who helped build it but got none of Mr. Poinsett's glory. The ghosts of the slaves who died during construction sometimes reappear as lights in the surrounding woods and on the bridge itself after dusk and hover in mid air for a few seconds and then vanish. One account of the haunting from the *Greenville News* suggests the lights are ghosts of Indians and Asians who helped to build the bridge. To my knowledge, Asian or Indian labor was not used in Upstate South Carolina, but as the legend states, an Indian burial mound was located nearby the site of the bridge and was destroyed in order to build the bridge. It could, then, be the souls of the displaced dead rising nightly at midnight to haunt the bridge. Screams have been heard near the site and some motorists have had difficulty starting their cars following a sighting.

I first discovered Poinsett Bridge as a Boy Scout looking for a thrill at Camp Old Indian. Between my interest in history and the rumors of ghost lights, the site was a natural attraction. It became a normal thing while camped at Old Indian to sneak out to the bridge to see the ghosts. Later I visited the site several times during my senior year of high school. I never had any car trouble, but I did hear a scream in the woods, which sent me back to the truck. I also saw the yellowish lights floating over the old abandoned stone bridge, which sent chills up my spine. I highly recommend a visit, both for the site's historical significance and its Hollywood-perfect atmosphere, especially at dusk on a rainy fall evening.

The "Devil's Castle": Just a spook story or the scariest place in Greenville?

The old tuberculosis (TB) hospital in Greenville County is better known as "Devil's Castle." According to some accounts, the building at some point served as an insane asylum. I could not verify this rumor, but given the nature of the haunting, it is a possibility. The haunting at "Devil's Castle" has caught the attention of many lovers of ghostlore, and the story was included in Terrance Zepke's 2004 book, *Best Ghost Tales of South Carolina*.

To understand why this and other TB hospitals might attract so many ghosts, an understanding of the disease and its early treatment is in order. Once the scourge of thousands of Americans, tuberculosis is a bacterial infection that attacks primarily the lungs. TB is transmitted through the air, a problem for those living with patients. Hence, the use of sanitariums or hospitals to house those diagnosed with the disease. Family and friends could visit with minimal risk of infection, but those who worked and lived in these hospitals were otherwise isolated from society. The loneliness and depression surely took a toll on those infected and isolated from normal life.

Thankfully, the 1950s saw the development of antibiotics that could fight the infection, ending the need for sanitariums and the isolation that accompanied them. The Greenville County Tuberculosis Hospital served the public from 1930 until the late 1950s. In the mid-1990s, following years of abandonment, the site of the former TB hospital became a work-release center for prisoners. Zepke claims that the site served as an insane asylum sometime between the late 1950s and the mid-1990s. By 1999, the site was again abandoned and the state and county began investigating other uses for the site. However, the legends surrounding the site made it an attractive hangout for teens and its isolation made it a haven for the homeless. In November 2002, a group of vagrants trying to keep warm started fires in paint cans. When these blazes got out of control, they destroyed the seventy-five-year old site. The ruins were bulldozed and a parking lot put in. No new development has been completed at the site as of May 2005.

The haunting at "Devil's Castle" first came to my attention when I was in high school in the late 1980s, while the site was between uses. The accounts of shadows dashing through the woods and screams in the night sucked me in and the site became a favorite spot for ghost hunting. Despite our reluctance to enter the site, my friends and I often saw figures in the trees and on the driveway. We also heard footsteps and other noises in the woods on many occasions. Either we were victims of groups with less regard for private property than we had, or the figures we saw—and some of them were prone to walk through obstacles any living person had to go around—were figments of the supernatural. We also heard stories about things being thrown at people without the help of human hands. The spot always gave us grounds for discussion and I looked forward to returning as a more responsible adult to do a more serious investigation. Unfortunately, I arrived at 220 Beverly Road in April 2005 to find a beautiful view, a new parking lot, and not much else; much to my dismay.

Willie Earle:
The beginning of his end

The lynching of Willie Earle has left its ghostly mark on two counties in South Carolina. Willie Earle was an ex-convict who was charged with the stabbing of a white cab driver named Brown in Greenville. (This is the only name listed in any of my sources.) Earle was arrested in Pickens County and held in the jail in Pickens while awaiting transport back to Greenville for trial.

According to the account given by Nancy Roberts, a Greenville cab driver named Johnny Worthington had shot and killed a black passenger in 1944 for talking back to him in answer to a stream of racial taunts. So Earle's attack on Brown could be considered retribution, or simply a robbery gone wrong, depending on one's point of view. In any event, Willie Earle was arrested in his hometown of Liberty in Pickens County, just over the line, immediately after the discovery of Brown's cab.

As soon as word got out of the arrest and Brown's fellow drivers found out that Earle was being held nearby, a lynch mentality took hold. According to Roberts's account, the group included Worthington, a man named Carlos Hurd and some others. Hurd knew the jailer in Pickens, a man named Gilstrap. At the same time, Willie Earle's mother had arrived at the jail to intercede on her son's behalf. She pointed out that Willie had less than three dollars with him when he was arrested, so he couldn't have robbed the driver, and that he had just returned from Virginia, making it unlikely that he was even in the state at the time of the crime and obviously had not benefited from it. It is unlikely that Mr. Gilstrap felt pity or even sympathy for Willie's mother, so he did nothing. Meanwhile, a caravan of taxis had formed in Greenville and was en route to Pickens. All the drivers had guns of some kind—shotguns, rifles or pistols. After midnight, the convoy arrived and the men demanded Gilstrap hand Willie Earle over.

After a very brief discussion, Gilstrap gave in to the group's demands and let them into the jail. An inmate, seeking to save his own skin, whether innocent or guilty, in a neighboring cell denied that he was the one they wanted and directed the men to Earle's cell. Willie Earle's protests of his innocence fell on deaf ears. The men drove him back to Greenville, to the Saluda Dam area near Bramlett Road. Upon arriving there, the cabbies confronted Earle about his crime. Despite his denials, twenty-six men rained blows all over his body, using fists, baseball bats and other weapons. After several minutes of this pummeling, Hurd or Worthington (or both) decided to go ahead and finish him off and shot Earle in the head twice.

Less than two days after Willie Earle's lynching, US Attorney General Tom Clark, a native Southerner, ordered FBI agents to Greenville to investigate the crime. The agents found twenty-six men willing to claim they had taken part in the attack. South Carolina Governor Strom Thurmond ordered the appointment of a special prosecutor to handle the trial of the men. The "poor whites" and "lintheads" cheered the men and their action, while upper-class whites were appalled. The jury consisted of twelve lower-class whites, who found all twenty-six accused not guilty. No one asked what the black community thought and they were not able to serve on the jury. The defense attorney, John B. Culbertson, was a noted liberal on civil rights for his time, but compared Earle to a mad dog in his closing argument.

My encounter with Willie Earle was planned in advance as an exercise in thrill-seeking, though we did not really expect to have an encounter. In my younger days, I attended church occasionally in Greenville and hung out with some friends who lived near Bramlett Road, which was the area where Willie Earle's body was eventually recovered. We read the account of the lynching in Nancy Roberts's book and decided to see for ourselves what might happen if we visited that spot. We called a cab to pick us up. The driver had no idea what our plan was. We asked to be driven to Pickens, and then return home. We gave the driver the address of the Pickens County Museum, which was originally the jailhouse where Earle had been imprisoned. We had an uneventful ride over and back.

Upon arriving back on Bramlett Road, though, we rolled down the windows in the backseat. As soon as the cab stopped, a low moan filled the air. The cabbie, realizing where he was, ordered us out of his cab with language I cannot repeat and took off like a scalded dog, leaving us on the side of the road about a half mile from my buddy's house. As we walked along, we laughed at the cabbie's fit of nerves as only smart-alecky teens can. As we walked, we kept up our joking at the cabbie's expense until the same low, rattling moan broke through the night air. We each accused the others for trying to scare us, and we each denied it. We soon decided that sitting in a well-lit room would be the best solution and we bolted.

Oddities and ends

Near Furman University, off US Highway 25 near Traveler's Rest, there is rumored to be a children's cemetery. Though the exact location of this long-abandoned burial site is unknown, local legends report lights seen both moving through the woods and hovering over graves. The laughter of children has been heard without a visible source. The sound of many people running has been heard as well as odd movements in the brush and nearby trees. According to this tale, most of the marked graves were for children and burials at the site stopped before 1900. Given the high infant and child mortality rates common at that time, I would not be surprised to eventually find the site.

South of the city of Greenville, in Mauldin, is NHC, a residential care facility for the elderly. . According to one local tale, some of the patients who have passed away have returned. One night, a nurse's aide on third shift saw a former resident who had died the night before walking down one of the halls in a long white nightgown. She did not mention the incident to her colleagues in order to avoid ridicule, until the night nurse returned from giving the dead woman's former roommate her medication. As the staffer was throwing the paper cup in the trash, the trashcan moved halfway across the floor. When the nurse asked if her aide had seen the trashcan move, the aide told her about her experience. The two staff members insisted on noting the events for the next shift in writing. The account does not say so, but I assume the record still exists in the company files, though when I called and asked about the incident no one knew anything about it and claimed that the records were off limits due to patients' privacy concerns.

Devenger Road is another haunted site in Greenville County. It is located near the town of Taylors in the community of Chick Springs on the east side of the county. The legend here is a modification of the cry baby bridge tale, best known from the school bus on the railroad tracks in South Texas where the victims of an earlier accident return. According to this version, a woman stopped on a bridge to get her kids something out of the trunk of her car on a long-ago Halloween night. A tractor-trailer came speeding along, didn't see the woman's car, and knocked it off the bridge into the creek below. Neither the mother nor her children survived. As with other accounts of this type, there is a ritual of sorts you have to follow to summon the ghosts on this cry baby bridge. You have to place your front two tires just over the hump of the bridge (likely the peak) and stop. Supposedly, your car will move backward and slightly up the hill, as if someone is trying to move your car. The legend claims the woman is trying to spare anyone else her fate.

Moonville is a community off US Highway 276 (Laurens Road) in the southeast corner of Greenville County. A Civil War cemetery is rumored to be just off US 276, on a dirt path to the right. If you go through the area at night, you will hear screams, loud breathing, the beating of drums and other strange noises. No apparitions have been reported.

LANCASTER COUNTY

Lancaster County is located in the north central part of South Carolina and is bordered by the state of North Carolina and Chester, York, Chesterfield, Fairfield and Kershaw Counties. The Catawba Indians thought of Lancaster County as part of their homeland and their settlement dates from 1000 BC. White settlement dates from about 1740. Lancaster was named for Lancaster, Pennsylvania, the area many of the early inhabitants first settled upon their arrival from Britain. The county was formed as one of the original counties of South Carolina in 1785, and was a hotbed of patriot activity in the Revolution. One of the four battles fought in the county, the massacre of Buford's command under a flag of truce, gave rise to a rallying cry heard at the victories of Cowpens and King's Mountain: "Buford's Quarter!"

During his tour of the South in 1791, President George Washington slept at three different sites in the county. All are marked with State Historic Markers. During the Civil War, troops under General Sherman passed through the southern part of the county during their advance from Columbia. Lancaster County was also the site of one of the only witch trials in the South in the early 1800s.

Lancaster County is the birthplace of the only US president born in South Carolina. Andrew Jackson was born in the Waxhaw Settlement in 1767, according to his own recollection, despite North Carolina's erroneous claims to the contrary. Lancaster County also gave South Carolina two governors, Jim Hodges and Stephen D. Miller. Stephen Miller also served as a US senator and was the father of Mary Boykin Chestnut, Civil War diarist and source for the book *A Diary from Dixie*.

Forty Acre Rock
(also known as Devil's Stomping Ground, South)

Forty Acre Rock is near the site of Buford's Massacre in Lancaster County. Colonel Abraham Buford led the 11th Virginia Regiment on the retreat from Charleston and Camden. Colonel Banastre Tarleton, a British cavalry leader and fierce foe of independence, caught up with the fleeing Americans in May 1780 and, legend has it, cut the survivors of his victory down under a flag of truce. American losses were over three hundred dead, wounded and captured, and the British lost just twenty men. According to local lore, the victims of Buford's Massacre were buried under Forty Acre Rock, giving rise to part of the ghostly legend of the site. The area is now under federal protection as a National Natural Landmark, so there has been no digging at the site to verify that claim.

The site has an area called the "Devil's Footprint" because of its resemblance to a giant footprint. The Waxhaw and Catawba tribes used this area as an execution site. According to legend, the spirits of the slain were collected by evil spirits and they have remained, waiting for the next time they are needed.

The haunted highlight of the area, however, is the "Devil's Stomping Ground." This is an apparently sterile spot of soil about forty feet across. It is surrounded by plants, and the woods and brush are full of insects and other life, but rarely are any bugs or animals, dead or alive, found in the bare spot. The name is derived from the belief that the devil uses the spot to contemplate what new mischief he will stir up. Based on the number of such sites all over the Western world, including one in nearby North Carolina, the devil has more thinking spots than there are Catholic Saints. The spot at Forty Acre Rock has been tested and proven to be scientifically sterile; one Internet source claims it is the oldest crop circle in the world. As with most sites rumored to be used as plotting areas by the devil (as well as some stone circles in Europe), objects left inside the circle overnight are found outside it the following morning.

In talking to Melody Craig, an expert on Lancaster County folklore, she told me that she had heard the stories about Forty Acre Rock since she was a girl, but had never had an experience there despite numerous visits. The only way to find out the truth is to go yourself. The site is worth a visit for the scenery alone.

Josh Log Road

This story came to my attention from Mrs. Melody Craig. She was polite enough to provide a typed version of the tale for my reference, and I thank her for her permission to use it. Josh Log Road is located in the community of Pleasant Plain, formerly Longville. It is haunted by the ghost of a blind elderly black man named Josh who played his fiddle while sitting on a fallen oak tree near his shack along the roadside in the years following the Civil War. Locals claimed that Josh could identify a person by the sounds of their wagon or footsteps. Josh was a community mascot, along with his pet bulldog. His neighbors took him food and generally took care of his needs.

One day, a passing stranger decided that Josh must be living on a hidden stash of funds and decided to lighten his load. The man beat Josh to death after attempting to locate his hidden (and non-existent) wealth and fled the area ahead of the posse that quickly formed.

Following his death, folks passing by Josh's old stomping ground began to see an old black man with snow-white hair near the old oak log and started hearing snatches of fiddle music after dark. The apparition only appeared to those on foot, which may explain why I was not fortunate enough to see anything the rainy night I drove through the area. Mrs. Craig said that she had not seen Josh either, but that she had heard the story since childhood and that occasionally she still hears reports of sightings in the area. So it may be worthwhile to stop by and take a short walk to stretch your legs. After all, SC 9 and SC 903 are both popular routes to Myrtle Beach and wouldn't a little fiddle music make the miles just fly by?

Gregory Graveyard:
Where they lie is known but to God
(and me, and I ain't telling)

The story of the haunting at the Gregory Family Cemetery is one I am reluctant to tell. Not because it is especially scary, but because I am loathe to encourage any more desecration of our historic cemeteries. Hence, my editorial decision not to include the exact location of the site.

The cemetery's first grave dates from 1785, as the Gregory family has very deep roots in Lancaster County. The haunting here is primarily auditory, with the sounds of children laughing and playing and a (very long-winded) preacher praying over a grave. According to one local legend, if you look carefully, you may see a path off to your left on your way out. It will not be visible on the way in. If you take this path, you may see the faces of those buried in the graves nearby. One version of this tale even goes so far to say that if you visit at midnight on Halloween the main path in will glow neon green.

On my visit to the site (to verify a grave's location for a library patron, not to see any ghosts), I was astonished to hear the sound of a child giggling in the woods. After a quick look to find my peeping tom, I found no one but myself. The experience, not to mention finding the grave I needed to fill my patron's request, made the trip worthwhile. Sadly, it wasn't Halloween, so I missed out on the path turning neon green.

LAURENS COUNTY

L aurens County is located in the western central part of South Carolina. It was formed in 1785 and is surrounded by Greenville, Spartanburg, Union, Newberry, Greenwood and Abbeville Counties. Laurens County was not a center of Native American life in early South Carolina, and the first white settlement dates from about 1770. The county was named for Henry Laurens, the first governor of South Carolina, president of the Continental Congress in 1777–78, and signer of the Treaty of Paris in 1783. He was exchanged for the British commander at Yorktown, Lord Cornwallis.

The county was the site of three Revolutionary battles. In late April 1865, Confederate President Jefferson Davis spent the night in the county while on the run from Union troops following Robert E. Lee's surrender. Two future governors of South Carolina, William D. Simpson and Robert A. Cooper, were born in Laurens County, as were Wil Lou Gray, the mother of adult education in South Carolina, and Ann Cunningham, founder of the Mount Vernon Ladies Association, which led the effort to preserve the home of George Washington. Following his escape from indenture, future President Andrew Johnson worked as a tailor in the town of Laurens before moving on to Tennessee.

One way to keep 'em out:
The lady of Lydia Mill

Lydia Mill is a mill village on the outskirts of Clinton, South Carolina. It is a typical example of an early twentieth-century planned mill community. After their heyday in the first half of the century, mill towns were great temptations for bored or nosy kids and one of the biggest problems theses cities face is keeping these kids out of the mill and off the railroad tracks that carry freight in and out of the mill. Lydia Mill has a natural defense against meddlesome pranksters—it's haunted.

According to legend, a woman was murdered on the site of the mill during construction in the late nineteenth century. She was beheaded and otherwise violated. A few days later, one of the workmen noticed that one of his colleagues was missing and then found her body. The attacker was never seen again, nor was the woman's head. The woman, however, was seen again. Her spectral form has been seen in the mill building, on the grounds and, especially, at the railroad tracks behind the mill.

I was eager to check this story out, given my interest in hauntings and the chance to see a headless woman float through a busy mill. So I called the Laurens County Library and asked if anyone there had heard the story. By luck, one of their regular patrons had worked at Lydia Mill for some forty years, on all shifts. The librarian I spoke to told me he would see if the gentleman would speak to me when he came in. The next day, I got a call from the librarian and the patron and grabbed a pen. Of course the scrap of paper with the gentleman's name on it has vanished, but I do greatly appreciate his kindness. He told me that the story was a put-on meant to keep nosy kids out of the mill and from getting hurt or worse. He said that despite living in the village for all of his life he had never seen the woman, but had heard the story since he was a babe. I thanked him for his help and still planned to drive through the area. A few weeks later, on the way back from Greenville, I found myself staying on I-385 toward I-26 and decided to check it out. I had hopes that I still might see something, but I had no such luck. Maybe this unfortunate woman was just a ruse, but I have not given up hope of glimpsing her headless form.

The body in the tunnel at Gray Court

This story consists of two very different versions. The version I heard from a native of Gray Court concerns a rape and murder victim whose body was found under a culvert (or tunnel) under I-385 near exit 10 (SC Highway 101). The girl's body was found after several days of exposure, which may explain her later appearance. Her attacker was never seen in the area again. The area around the culvert is well known in town as a necking spot and if you are not careful, the girl's ghost may appear. She enjoys pressing her face against steamed-up windows while beating her fists on the car roof. Her face is noteworthy for the lack of complete features: one eye is absent, as is most of her lower jaw. She has also been known to cause cars not to crank and have other electrical or mechanical failures. The speculation in Gray Court is that she wants to save other teenage girls from her fate. This version does not place the ghost in the culvert, but on the nearby frontage road.

The second version of this story credits the haunting to the murder of an elderly woman by a neighborhood boy who visited under the presence of borrowing some eggs. Under the mistaken impression that the lady had some money stashed away, he hit her to make her talk while on the way to the henhouse. Sadly, he hit her frail frame too hard and she fell dead at the culvert, which is located near the site of the old lady's chicken coop. According to this tale, if you enter the tunnel on rainy days, you will hear her cries of pain. The site also says that if you drive into the tunnel and cut you car off, it will not restart and that the woman may appear in your car.

Back to cry baby bridge— this one over the Enoree

Yes, here's another version of a cry baby bridge. This version dates back to the end of the Civil War, after the burning of Columbia, when General Sherman was a terror. A group of refugees from the Columbia area heard a rumor that Sherman was coming up toward Greenville and would burn all the towns and railroad bridges en route. Instead, Sherman veered to the eastern part of the state and only an occasional patrol came through the area. Of course, in wartime, rumors are as true as facts and these exhausted folks fled north toward Spartanburg. They decided to hide under the railroad trestle over the Enoree River.

A young mother and her baby were with the refugee party. In order to avoid attention from the approaching troops (though as it turned out, there were none), the mother kept her hand over the baby's mouth to keep it from crying. By morning, the baby had suffocated. The party tried to bury the child and move on, but the mother lost her mind and refused to allow anyone near her baby. The party continued on, only to look back and watch the mother leap from the trestle to the river below with her child in her arms. When the refugees reached the riverbank, only the lifeless child could be found floating in the current. Today, as legend has it, if you walk across the trestle or the nearby highway bridge, a woman in an old-fashioned dress may join you. You may also be able to hear the soft, muffled cries of a baby.

One day in March 2005 I decided to check this story out for myself. US Highway 221 goes over the Enoree, right next to a railway trestle, and that is the bridge I chose to explore. I arrived at the bridge about eight o'clock that night. Thankfully, traffic was non-existent, and I decided to walk across, making as much noise as possible so that anyone listening would know they had an audience. I got about halfway over before I heard the soft sobbing of a child. I must confess, having expected to hear nothing, I panicked and sprinted back to my car. A few Johnny Cash songs later, I decided to walk up to the tracks and see if I could stir up the mother as well. There is a signal visible from the trestle that allowed me to determine that the tracks were clear for the time being. I decided to chance it, but did not want to tarry, as trains sometimes do run on time. After a quick glance to see the lay of the land, I took off, taking two sets of tracks at the time. I quickly crossed the river and headed right back across. I saw or heard nothing unusual, thankfully. I doubt my heart could have taken it if I had.

NEWBERRY COUNTY

N ewberry County is located in the central part of the state and is bordered by Union, Fairfield, Lexington, Saluda, Greenwood and Laurens Counties. There is not much of a Native American presence left in the county, as whites first settled it in the late 1740s. German Lutherans settled in the area, with a scattering of English settlers as well.

Newberry County was established in 1785 and was named for a Captain John Newberry, an early settler who served with General Thomas Sumter in the Revolution. There were eight Revolutionary battles fought in the county. In 1791, Methodist Bishop Francis Ashbury passed through the area sowing the seeds of a still-thriving Methodist community. There were no Civil War battles fought in Newberry County, though the commander of a group of US colored troops did order the execution of a former Confederate private there following an assault on one of his men in September 1865. The county was a hotbed of Klan activity during Reconstruction, and several black officeholders and their supporters were murdered. Newberry County was the home or birthplace of two governors of South Carolina and three US senators, James Henry Hammond, William Harper and Coleman Blease. Hammond and Blease held both offices.

Newberry College:
A ghost for every building (almost)

The Lutheran Church established Newberry College in 1856. During the Civil War, the college was used as a Confederate hospital and, immediately after the war, as a US Army garrison. The college relocated to Walhalla in Oconee County from 1868 to 1877, returning with the end of Republican rule. In fact, the best-known ghost story on the campus dates back to the period of its use as a hospital and garrison.

Before the Civil War, a young man named John from Wisconsin fell in love with a local belle named Madeline. With the coming of conflict, John returned north to fight, while Madeline stayed in Newberry to roll bandages for the Confederacy. When the US Army took over the campus following the war, John returned to Newberry with his unit. Madeline hoped they would rekindle their affair and John encouraged this hope. However, in 1877, John left Newberry with his unit without even a farewell for Madeline. Madeline climbed the belfry tower in Keller Hall in hopes to catch John's attention as he rode past. However, failing to get any response from her departing lover, she wrapped the bell rope around her neck and hung herself in despair. As she fell, the bell rang out.

When a doctor examined her body, he determined that the fall was not lethal and that her neck was not broken. The official cause of death was listed as a broken heart. After students returned to the campus in 1877, the bell in Keller Hall would ring out one time every autumn without the help of human hands.

After co-education arrived at Newberry in the 1920s, an enterprising male student started the tradition known as Madeline's return. A male student would ring the bell in Keller Hall, shouting "Don't fall in love with a Yankee!" while another, dressed in drag, ran to Smeltzer Hall, which was the female dormitory. In a 1986 article, the return of this tradition was rumored, despite the removal of the bell from Keller Hall to a trailer on campus. Not withstanding the occasional prank, people still hear the bell ring out over the campus on fall nights.

The second ghost at Newberry College can be found on the second floor of Kinard Hall, a dormitory on campus. Students have reported poltergeist activity there year-round. Incidents include faucets turning on by themselves, windows opening without help and cabinet drawers and closet doors flying open. No suicides or other tragedies have marred the building's history. I could not gain access to Kinard Hall and none of the people I spoke to on campus had heard anything about any poltergeist activity there.

The "happy" Hound of Goshen: First look

The story of the Hound of Goshen extends over parts of two counties. We will merely introduce the topic here. The Hound of Goshen has been seen since the mid-1850s along Maybinton Road, which was once part of the main stagecoach route from Columbia to the mountains of North Carolina, and was once known as the Old Buncombe Road. The large amount of traffic on this road attracted peddlers and other, less reputable people who liked to prey on unwary and exhausted travelers. Back in the early 1850s, a faithful hound accompanied one of these peddlers on his rounds. However, this man's success in separating travelers from parts of their bankrolls attracted the attention of some locals with the intention of taking the stolen goods for themselves. They surprised the sleeping peddler near the plantation of a Dr. Douglas. After a brief struggle, the locals gained the peddler's ill-gotten gains and headed to the nearest grog seller's.

The peddler's hound began to howl and the mournful baying attracted Dr. Douglas's attention. He quickly came and offered what help he could before the beating took its ultimate toll. The hound refused to leave its master's side, even after his interment in a nearby potter's field. After a few days, the hound died from starvation and exposure.

The people who lived nearby forgot about the incident until a few months later, when stage drivers and other travelers reported being chased by a spectral hound that stood as high as a calf and even kept up with stages drawn by six horses at full gallop through some heavy brush. The hound always vanished at the gate of the Douglas plantation. Over the years, the hound has been sighted along the length of Maybinton Road, appearing and vanishing without a sound.

I have seen the Hound of Goshen many times over the years. My first encounter with the hound came when I was in high school. I had driven to

Columbia from my home in Lyman for a political event. Even then I would much rather drive a back road than an interstate highway, especially if the whitetail deer weren't in mating season and would be less likely to jump in front of my speeding car. I decided that a shortcut cutting the corner off US Highway 176 toward Union would be both scenic and faster. It was about nine o'clock on a chilly March night when I turned onto what was then Old Buncombe Road. After passing Brazelmans Bridge Road, I noticed a large white shape in the woods to my left. I slowed down, trying to figure out what it was. I lost sight of it for a second, and when it reappeared, it was right behind me and gaining. I saw that it was a large white hound and decided it would eventually give up the chase and go home. After about a quarter mile, I noticed it was still there. It was then I realized what road I was on and what was chasing me. I then floored the gas and hoped to find a gas station. Before I hit the Union County line, the hound was gone.

The rider of Bush River

This story dates back to the days of the partisan warfare that racked the Upstate of South Carolina during the Revolution. It is also one of the oldest documented stories I found, given that it first appeared in print in a Columbia newspaper in 1860, according to Nancy Roberts. The story is one of lost love and the personal impact of war.

Young Henry Galbreath and Charity Miles were lovers and were eagerly awaiting their coming wedding when Charleston fell in 1780. As the British moved to consolidate their control of the colony, young men were forced to take sides. Even Charity's Quaker father understood when Henry told Charity he was going to join the patriot cause. Henry promised to return in a year, dead or alive. Charity promised to wait for him and marry no other. She followed his exploits with Colonel William Washington's colonial cavalry from those who returned home wounded. As the year came to a close, Charity eagerly scanned the faces of those passing by her log home on Bush River, near Bobo's Mills.

Following the American victory at Cowpens, news of her beloved became scarce. One night in December 1781, at about two in the morning, Charity was awakened by the fast approach of a single rider. Dashing to the door, she saw a man ride past on a snow-white stallion. As she approached, she saw the dozens of bullet holes in his long black cape and knew without seeing his face who it was. The rider glowed in the gloom and no tracks or other signs were ever seen. Even after Charity's death as an old widow, the rider still galloped past, though sometimes only the sound of horse's hooves and a faint glow were present.

I rode down to Bush River to try to find any trace of either Bobo's Mills or the rider himself. I decided to start my hunt in the community of Bush River. There was no mention of Bobo's Mills on the 1825 Mills Atlas of South Carolina, the oldest source for the sites of old mills and farms. I also could not locate a Miles homestead in the area, but I knew that the Miles and Galbreath families had migrated to Ohio from the Newberry area by 1830. I decided Garys Road would be my best bet, since it crosses Bush River and was suitably remote. I arrived about midnight, thinking that traffic would be nil and I would be lucky. Despite the ground mist and noise of tree frogs and the trees lining the edge of the dark road, no hoofbeats or faint glows disturbed the night. I'm not sure if I was in the wrong place at the wrong time, but I think there's a good chance that Henry Galbreath still rides. I just have to track him down.

The Bride of West End:
For single men only

The Bride of West End apparently only appears to single men, which may explain some of the difficulty I had in finding her. According to the legend, the ghost appears in the form of a dreary lady in a wedding dress sitting in the trees. She has also been seen standing near her grave, though her name and the location of her grave are unknown, or walking the nearby streets and fields. She is supposed to be waiting for her lover to come and finish their elopement. He left her at the altar, causing her to die of a broken heart.

OCONEE COUNTY

O conee County is located in the northwest corner of the state and is bordered by the states of North Carolina and Georgia, and Pickens and Anderson Counties. Oconee County was part of the homeland of the Cherokee Indian tribe for millennia until the arrival of whites in the mid 1500s. After finally allowing white settlement in the late 1750s, the growth of tensions led to the Cherokee War of 1760–61. The Cherokee War largely broke the power of the Cherokee, though the final blow did not come until the campaign of 1776–77. One of the principal towns of the Cherokee tribe, Keowee, was in what is now Oconee County.

Three Revolutionary War battles were fought in the county. William Bartram, noted early American naturalist, visited the area in 1776, painting pictures and getting samples of the wildlife. The area was reserved as Indian territory until the formation of Pendleton County in 1789. The area now encompassing Oconee County was part of Pendleton County until the formation of Pickens County in 1826. Oconee County was not formally established until the ratification of the Constitution of 1868.

In 1938, the first soil conservation district plan in America was put in place in Oconee County. The name Oconee was derived from a Cherokee term, "Uk-oo-na," which means the place of springs. No South Carolina senators or governors have called Oconee County home as yet. The county is known for its mountain scenery and is the site of Lake Keowee.

Larry Stephens still needs a ride on Route 107

According to local lore, Larry Stephens was a young pilot who kept a small plane at the Greenville airport in the 1950s. Stephens especially enjoyed flying over the lakes and mountains of Oconee County. Late one afternoon, Stephens realized that the weather had changed and that his fuel would not be sufficient to get him back to Greenville. As hail hammered his small craft and the wind screamed around the cockpit, Larry began to seek a safe spot to ride out the storm. He saw the thin ribbon of asphalt that marked South Carolina Highway 107. He hoped to ride his remaining fuel down and then figure out how to get his plane back out later. However, his engine shuddered to a stop before he could correct his course and the plane crashed into the side of a mountain. The body of the plane was almost completely destroyed, and his body was never found.

Shortly after the recovery of Stephens's plane, a man began to show up just after dark on rainy or stormy nights on SC 107 between the Piedmont Overlook and Moody Springs, hitching a ride. If the car is going south, the rider gets out at Moody Springs. If north, he gets out at the Overlook. He always wears a loose-fitting, dark-colored, all-weather jacket that might have been leather before mud and the elements took their toll. Once in the car, the man does not speak after he states his destination. The man is reported to leave a puddle of muddy water in the seat of the car and does not acknowledge the poor driver who stopped in such nasty weather with even a wave—mainly because he vanishes right after he exits the car. The former superintendent of Oconee State Park, Bob Cothran, has heard the same story over the last fifty years and is convinced that the hitchhiker is none other than Larry Stephens.

After reading an account of this story in Nancy Roberts's *Ghosts of the Carolinas* as a nine-year-old thrill seeker, I decided that one of first trips after getting my driver's license would be to SC 107. As it happened, I didn't get a chance to go until I was a freshman in college. I spent the weekend camping at Table Rock State Park and decided to ride up SC 107 after stopping in Walhalla for supper one rainy Saturday night. The further I drove, the worse the storm got. By the time I reached Moody Springs, hail was falling and the rain was so hard I could barely see my high beams in the darkness. I decided to pull off and ride out the worst of the weather, and then head back to my soggy tent.

After being parked for about two or three minutes, I noticed a man standing alone in the rain, looking off into the trees below. I called out and asked if he needed a ride. I must confess that Larry Stephens was the last thing on my mind at that moment; I just saw a fellow human being who might need a hand. He said he needed a ride and walked over. I opened the door and saw that he was soaked to the skin and muddy. I asked if he had been caught by the storm, but his only reply was a request to be let out at the Piedmont Overlook. Surprised, I stopped talking and started the car. After a few minutes' drive, I reached the Overlook and pulled over. Without a word, the man got out, took a step back toward the road and vanished. Needless to say, I did not drive back to my tent. I sped back to Walhalla and found a well-lit motel and for the first and last time as an adult, slept with all the lights on. I must say, the forty bucks for the room was the best money I have ever spent.

PICKENS COUNTY

The state of North Carolina as well as Anderson, Oconee and Greenville Counties border Pickens County. Pickens County served as a major part of the Cherokee homeland from about 1000 BC up to the start of English settlement around 1750. The area also served as a focal point of the conflict in the Cherokee War of 1760–61, along with its future neighbor Oconee. Pickens County was the home base of the Revolutionary patriot leader Andrew Pickens, better known as the Wizard Owl, who also gave his name to the county. The county was the site of two Revolutionary battles.

Pickens County sent General Pickens's son, Andrew Pickens Jr., to the governor's chair, along with the general's grandson, Francis W. Pickens, who served as South Carolina's governor during secession and the firing on Fort Sumter. Pickens County was officially formed in 1826 from the former Pendleton County. It was also the home of John C. Calhoun, from his election as vice president in 1825 to his death in 1850. Calhoun twice served as US senator, secretary of both state and war and as a congressman. John Ewing Colhoun also served as a US senator from Pickens County.

Hester Store in Dacusville

The haunting at Hester Store in Dacusville concerns a lynching victim who was hung at the rear of the building from an old oak tree. It is said that on certain nights, you can see his body swaying from a branch in a long-gone breeze. Also visible at times is an old woman in a rocking chair seen in one of the second-story windows. One version claims this is the ill-fated lover of the lynching victim, who truly loved the man despite the racial chasm between them. Another version claims that the lady in the rocker is the mother of the victim. My visits to Hester Store did not help solve the riddle, however.

I have visited Hester Store on two different occasions, and twice came away disappointed. The first visit came on a side trip while hiking near Caesars Head State Park. I stopped in on a whim, but had heard the story from a high school friend in Greenville. I paid for my cigarettes and asked the lady behind the counter if she had seen the man hanging behind the store lately. Perhaps put off by my three-day stubble and dirty shorts, she said nope and tossed my change at me. Since it was mid-afternoon and I had not made the best first impression, I decided not to hang around until dark to see for myself. I long regretted the missed opportunity.

A second chance presented itself when doing research for this book. After visiting sites in Greenville, Union and Newberry Counties, I remembered Hester Store and headed to Pickens. I arrived at the site at about five-thirty in the afternoon. Sadly, it was midspring and darkness was still a few hours away. I ran in to ask about the continued presences on the site and to see if I could hang around and get some pictures. Sadly, and according to my luck, the lady behind the counter was new to the area and had not heard either story. She was not very excited about having a stranger hanging around waiting for a ghost, especially since it would not be dark for a good three hours, so I left, cursing my missed opportunity.

Pickens County Museum:
The end of Willie Earle and typhoid

According to local lore, Willie Earle still maintains a presence at the old Pickens County Jail, now the Pickens County Museum. Though he was lynched in

Greenville and some say his ghost haunts a deserted stretch of road there, some others have reported seeing the face of a terrified young black man staring out from a first-floor window on cloudy February nights.

However, there are other souls who are still calling this building home despite their passing from this world. Typhoid fever was a scourge in the South at the turn of the last century, at times wiping out whole families. This misfortune struck the family of the first sheriff to live in the building in 1903. According to legend, the matriarch of this family still looks after her children in the building, and some say still looks out on the changing face of her hometown.

The woman was Sarah McDaniel, the wife of James McDaniel, the first resident sheriff in the then new building. It was a fairly common practice at the time to allow the jailer and his family to stay there in lieu of having to pay rent elsewhere. However, the family also suffered some of the same hardships as their unwilling houseguests. Shortly after the opening of the new jail, sewage backed up into the building and the well also. Five of the fifteen family members (thirteen of them children) died of typhoid. Sarah was the last of the five to die. According to local lore and an article from the *Greenville News*, Sarah McDaniel was so attached to her children that she could not bear to leave her surviving children in their hour of need.

Workers in the upstairs gallery of the museum have complained of papers vanishing and later reappearing in odd places and hearing footsteps after hours. Passersby have also seen a figure staring from an upstairs window after closing. However, this may be Willie Earle looking for someone to come spare him from his fate.

My visit to the Pickens County Museum was fruitful in terms of photographs, but not in terms of actual sightings. When I arrived one afternoon, I was surprised to find the museum closed for remodeling. I snapped some photographs anyway, and returned home disappointed. However, after we came home, my friend Michael Ravenel looked over the prints of my photographs. He was rather surprised to see a face in the upstairs window of the exterior shot of the museum.

SPARTANBURG COUNTY

Spartanburg County is in the northern part of the Upstate. It is surrounded by the state of North Carolina and Cherokee, Union, Laurens and Greenville Counties. The area now known as Spartanburg County was first settled by Native Americans before 1000 BC, with whites entering the area by the late 1740s. The western part of the county was the site of several battles between whites and Native Americans during the Cherokee War. Fort Prince, near Wellford, was a camp for the militia taking part in the 1776 expedition against the Cherokee that cleared the area of most of the resident Native Americans.

The county was the site of ten Revolutionary War battles—the most in the Upstate—including the battle of Cowpens. Spartanburg County was officially formed in 1785 and included part of what is now Cherokee County, formed in 1897. It was named for the Spartan Regiment, which was a local unit that took part in several Revolutionary campaigns. As befits a place with such a long military heritage, Camp Wadsworth in World War I and Camp Croft in World War II served as massive infantry training centers.

Spartanburg County has given South Carolina four governors: Ibra Blackwood, Olin D. Johnston, Donald Russell and James F. Byrnes. Olin Johnston was born in Anderson County but called Spartanburg home. All of these, except Blackwood, also served as United States senators from South Carolina. Byrnes also served as secretary of state under President Truman and briefly as associate justice to the US Supreme Court. Olin Johnston's daughter Elizabeth Patterson was the first female elected to represent South Carolina in the US House of Representatives. Spartanburg County was the site of the first erosion control project in the Southeast, and is a major industrial and educational center in South Carolina.

Foster's Tavern

Foster's Tavern was placed on the National Register of Historical Places in 1970. The building was built about 1807 and is one of the oldest remaining brick houses in the Upstate. Today it is a private residence.

John C. Calhoun was a frequent guest during his service in Washington, owing to the building's location at the intersection of roads leading to Charleston, North Carolina and Georgia.

The haunting at Foster's Tavern has only been reported in local media since the 1980s, but has been around since the turn of the century. The oddest aspect of the haunting is the sound of horses' hooves on the roof. Also troubling to residents is the piano, which has been played by invisible hands and does not stay in one place after being moved to a new location in the room. Voices and footsteps have also been heard at night.

Since the tavern is now a private residence, I could not gain access to prove or disprove any occurrences, but I will share one odd event I witnessed. I was born and raised in Spartanburg County and grew up hearing legends of the haunting at the tavern. After college I lived in a former mill community named Glendale, which is near Foster's Tavern. Since I drove SC Highway 295 quite often between my parents' home in Lyman and my apartment in Glendale, I passed the site at least once a week. One night, as I sat at the red light at the intersection of SC 295 and SC Highway 56, I glanced toward the large brick building on my right and wondered if anyone still lived there. Almost in answer to my question, a woman's pale face appeared in the glass panel of the door I was looking at. Thankfully, the light changed and I took advantage of my place at the front of the pack. The house was occupied at that time, but the fact that I could see the wall *through* her gave credence to the stories I had heard. I would urge readers to remember that though Foster's Tavern is on the National Register of Historic Places, it is a private residence. Please respect the owners' privacy.

Creepy colleges:
Wofford, Converse, Spartanburg Technical and Spartanburg Methodist

These four colleges have a special place in my heart and in the hearts of members of my family. I am a proud graduate of both Spartanburg Methodist and Wofford Colleges, as is my grandfather. My father graduated from Spartanburg Methodist with me in 1992, the only time in the school's history father and son have walked in the same class. My father and younger brother also attended Spartanburg Technical College for a brief time, my brother in the 1990s and my father in the 1970s. My grandmother, mother and younger sister all graduated from Converse College, all at different times. Of all the ghost stories at these four different campuses, the only one to come to my attention from a non-family member was the haunting at Spartanburg Technical College.

Wofford College is home to three different ghosts. The college was founded in 1859 by the United Methodist Church. The first haunting can be found in the auditorium in the Old Main Building, which is both the focal point of and the oldest building on campus. I discovered this occurrence, known to students as "Ole Green Eyes," during my senior year, with my good friend, Phillip Stone, who is now the archivist at Wofford. We entered the auditorium one night during our last semester on campus. During the Civil War, Old Main served as a hospital for the Confederacy. According to the legend, a Yankee prisoner of war died at Old Main toward the end of the war and vowed to return to the scene of his death every year. The date of his return varies depending on who you talk to, but we had been told that early March was our best bet to see anything unusual. We were told to keep an eye on the top edge of the drapes over the large windows on the outer wall. Sure enough, about halfway back from the stage, we saw two small green lights appear in space. My first reaction was to open the drapes and look for another light source or a prankster. Nothing was visible but the bulk of the library next door, and the two small lights were still there, despite the additional light. We hung around for a few more minutes and the two spots remained visible as we left.

The second ghost on campus is found at the DuPre house, now part of the administration building. According to Doyle Boggs, director of communications for the college, the ghost is known as "Uncle Dan" and is reputed to be Professor D.A. DuPre, who was raised in the house and taught and lived at Wofford from 1872 to 1930. The haunting manifests as a friendly presence that is concerned about employees who are working late.

The final ghost at Wofford is found in the Carlisle-Wallace House, home of the dean of the college. This building dates to the Civil War and served as part of the hospital on the campus. People have reported hearing footsteps upstairs at night, despite there being no one upstairs. Boggs believes the haunting is explained by the desire of the dead soldiers to return to duty. I asked my old friend Phillip Stone if, as the college archivist, he had come across any firsthand accounts or other information on these hauntings and he said no to both requests.

Converse College is a women's college founded in 1889 by Dexter Converse, a pioneer in the local textile industry. There have been six different ghosts reported on campus. The journal *Names in South Carolina* claims that Mr. Converse haunts the campus that bears his name. According to the 1975 article, Mr. Converse was originally buried on campus but his wife had him reinterred in a nearby cemetery. His ghost reappeared to check on the campus and the students.

Wilson Hall, the oldest building on campus, is home to two other ghosts, one in the Hazel Abbott Theater and one in the bell tower. According to some accounts, the ghost in the Abbott Theater is Mrs. Abbott herself. Witnesses have complained of noises in the prop storage room, missing or relocated props and disembodied footsteps and voices heard both backstage and in the seats. Supposedly, if you sit in Mrs. Abbott's seat, she will haunt you. The tale gives no details of what happens when she haunts you or even which seat should be avoided, however. My mother was fairly active in the theater while she was a student at Converse and she recalled hearing about the ghost then. She did not have any unusual experiences, however. When I contacted the college archives, no one in that office had any information on the haunting in the theater.

The other haunt in Wilson Hall is found in the bell tower, which is one of the main landmarks on campus. According to legend, two men had a fight on the stairway leading to the top of the tower sometime just after its construction. One of the men was either pushed or slipped to his death.

The other ghosts on campus are found in residence halls. Pell Hall is home to two ghosts, one merely seen and one seen and heard. The ghost that is only seen is supposed to be Betty Payne, who committed suicide in her room in the 1950s by hanging. The room is no longer used to house students, but you can supposedly see the outline of her hanging body and the noose on the door.

Some people claim that a demonic face is also visible on the door. The images have supposedly remained despite all attempts to remove them, including repainting, scraping and finally replacing the door in question. The ghost is prone to lock people in her old room and has a reputation of being hostile. Sadly, the Spartanburg newspaper did not have an obituary for anyone named Betty Payne during the 1950s and the Converse archives had no information on any deaths in Pell Hall. My grandmother had not heard the story during her time on campus and my mother and sister had not as well, but since they commuted to school and did not live in the dorm that may be why.

The final ghost to be found at Converse is in Williams Hall, which was built in the 1950s. A boy came to visit his sister and was unfortunately killed on the way. His ghost has supposedly taken up residence in the laundry room in Williams Hall and is said to be kind and gentle. No one I spoke to could remember having any encounters or having heard the story.

Spartanburg Technical College was built in the late 1960s to retrain textile workers in different fields and to provide an alternative to the standard college experience for workers and other untraditional students. It was located in an industrial corridor along I-85, now I-85 Business, on land that was once the site of the County Prison Farm. My father and my brother have attended classes at Tech, as it is known in the area, but this haunting came to my attention from John Wylder, a friend of mine who used to work at the school library.

The haunting is focused at the library and dates back to the last days of the County Prison Farm. According to one account, two inmates had a fight and one man lost. His body was discovered on the site of the current college library, and he is responsible for the banging and other noises that are said to come from the building after hours. Another version of this tale credits the haunting to an early library employee who died suddenly at home. According to this tale, the ghost of this man is the source of the banging noises and scattered sightings of a figure in the building as well. Mr. Wylder himself (as well as my father and brother) never saw anything unusual, but campus security has had difficulties with their communications equipment in the library, including calls from a locked and secure building and odd occurrences of interference.

Spartanburg Methodist College was founded by Dr. David Camak in 1911. According to local legends, Willard Hall, one of the men's dorms on campus, is haunted by a student who jumped to his death from his room window. Though the identity of this man and the date of his death are unknown, the figure of the man is said to appear in the window of his former room, as well as in the halls of the dorm.

Walnut Grove Plantation:
Worth a visit, but (maybe?) not for the ghost

The haunting at Walnut Grove Plantation dates back to the early 1780s and the internecine strife of the Revolution. Walnut Grove belonged to the Moore family from 1763 until it was given to the Spartanburg County Historical Association. A Captain Steadman of the local patriot militia is said to have died at the plantation from his wounds suffered in a Tory raid by "Bloody Bill" Cunningham. Modern caretakers and housekeepers have complained of finding a man-size depression in the mattress in one bedroom, despite the feather bed having been fluffed the night before. An odd glow has been spotted in the bedrooms on dark evenings, also.

Sadly, one of the best-known aspects of the haunting has been discredited with the passage of time. The "eternal bloodstain" that was said to have marked where the valiant captain fell has been exposed as a fake. According to an e-mail I received from Becky Slayton, administrator of the plantation, an early curator placed the stains on the floor in order to increase interest when the house was opened to the public in the 1960s. However, Ms. Slayton did add that she had seen lights near the Moore family cemetery on the grounds, despite there not being any power in the area or any light source.

I have my own reason for believing in the haunting at Walnut Grove. My parents always encouraged me and my siblings to explore our world and they also encouraged our interests. Since one of my major interests was history, we made a point of visiting historic sites both great and small. On one of these summertime field trips, when I was about eleven, my parents and I visited Walnut Grove. During the tour, I got bored and slipped upstairs. On entering one of the bedrooms, I saw a depression on the bed. It was about the size of a man—about 5'10" or so. As I stood there, mouth agape, I heard footsteps going to the window across from me. When the footsteps stopped, I came to my senses and bolted back downstairs. I have not been back to Walnut Grove since.

Schoolhouse spooks: Broome High School and South Carolina School for the Deaf And Blind

Sadly, none of the public schools I attended in Spartanburg County had resident ghosts. Luckily, two schools I have ties to do, though I discovered one after my chance for any in-depth onsite investigation had passed. The school in question is Broome High School on the east side of the county. The legend is a sad one. During the school's construction, one of the roofers brought his daughter to work with him. The girl was on the roof with her father and wandered too close to the edge and fell to her death. According to the tale, the girl still screams for her father in the night.

I wish I had known the full story when I was in college. My then girlfriend was an alumna of Broome High and once told me that she had had a traumatic experience after school one night. She had dropped her car off at the school to meet a date for the evening. They returned from their date about midnight and were greeted by the unmistakable cries of a young girl looking for her father. Thinking some mutual friends had decided to play a prank, they looked for anyone else in vain. The cries continued until my friend bolted for her car and returned home. After that night, she refused to go back on the grounds after dark unless she was surrounded by a large number of friends. The Spartanburg School District Three Office has no information on either the haunting or the death of any child during the school's construction. The Spartanburg County Library had no information in their collection, either.

I have a much more personal connection to the other haunted school in Spartanburg. My mother has worked at the South Carolina School for the Deaf and Blind (SCSDB) for ten years in various capacities. SCSDB was founded in 1849 by Reverend Newton P. Walker and his wife Martha. The state took the school over in 1856 and construction began on the main building, Walker Hall, in 1858. The Walkers remained to guide the school. Reverend Walker died in 1861 and his widow Martha kept the school open until 1866. SCSDB was closed from 1866 to 1869 due to the state's poor financial condition. In 1872, the Reconstruction legislature ordered SCSDB to be integrated. The school closed after a mass resignation of the faculty, until 1876 when it was reopened with separate departments for whites and blacks. The school finally integrated permanently in 1966, without incident. From 1999 to 2003, Walker Hall underwent extensive renovation and now serves as the administrative center of the campus. Walker Hall was placed on the National Register of Historical Places in 1977.

Members of the Walker family held either the superintendence or presidency of SCSDB from 1849 to 1980, with a brief period from 1869 to 1872 when John Hughston was superintendent. Martha Walker acted as superintendent from Reverend Walker's death in 1861 until 1869. The Walker family maintained apartments in Walker Hall from its opening in 1861 until Martha's death in 1900. These apartments were located in the east wing of the building and have served as a focal point for the haunting.

The ghost of Walker Hall is none other than Martha Walker. She is not especially frightening; no screams or eternal bloodstains mar her legacy. Mrs. Walker is simply making sure her former home and the students once under her care are thriving.

Martha Walker has been seen by several students and staff members of SCSDB. Lawrence Sloan, a graduate of the School for the Deaf, was sorting photographs for the museum one day in 1980 when he thought someone was in the hall outside on the second floor. He first thought he was the victim of a prank, but as soon as he saw the woman's face, he knew it was Martha Walker. Fearing ridicule, Mr. Sloan held his tongue until his retirement in 1989, when he mentioned that he had had an experience of his own in response to a question from a colleague. Kathy Brown, whom I did not get to interview, felt a rush of wind on the third floor while working alone and heard a locked door close, according to Mr. Sloan. Mr. Sloan is very proud of his alma mater and place of employment, and it showed in his pride of place during our interview. Lisa Bowen saw a shadow from the corner of her eye in the gift shop on the first floor following the renovation of the building. Mrs. Bowen did not see the face of her specter, but believes it was Mrs. Walker. During my visit, Mrs. Bowen told me that one of her coworkers had witnessed a seeing-eye dog just out of training raise its hackles outside her third-floor office. Seeing-eye dogs are chosen for their even temperament; for one to respond to a non-evident stimulus is very unusual. Mary Washko, another current SCSDB employee, saw a woman in an old-fashioned brown formal dress on the east side of the third floor prior to the renovation. She thought that it might be a visiting trustee and went to offer her assistance. By the time she reached the stairway, the woman had vanished and there was no trace of her anywhere. From that vantage you could see from the third floor to the first easily.

These stairs also figured in my personal experience with Martha Walker. When I was in college, I took two basic sign language classes at Walker Hall, prior to the renovation. I must confess I retained none of it, but I enjoyed the experience. The classes started at eight at night and ran from November to March. As my readers know, it gets late early out there at that time of the year. I arrived on campus before class one day, about seven thirty, hoping to look around Walker Hall and see if I could find the ghost I felt sure called the building home. Imagine my surprise at seeing a lady on the stairs above me. All I saw was a flash of brown fabric, and I heard the rustle of old-fashioned petticoats and soft footsteps before I reached the second-floor landing. No one was visible at all. I wish my sign language skill had been good enough to have asked the instructor about my experience. I urge everyone to visit SCSDB for the beauty of the campus, the skill and caring of the staff, the achievement of the students and, if you are lucky, the concern of a long-dead superintendent.

Oakwood Cemetery and the Tanning Yards

Oakwood Cemetery was the first cemetery I ever played in as a child and is probably to blame for my current job as local history coordinator and "the cemetery man," where I deal so often with locating graves of ancestors for researchers. The Tanning Yards were a favorite spot to drink, chat, and basically hang out in college and is still the most scenic spot between my home in Chester and my parents' home in Lyman.

Oakwood Cemetery is one of the older cemeteries in the city of Spartanburg. It is located in the Converse Heights neighborhood about two blocks from the campus of Converse College. According to the legend of the haunting, lights have been seen in the woods surrounding the cemetery. Cellular phones and digital cameras have been known to malfunction while inside the cemetery, only to return to normal after leaving. A white mist and apparitions of children have been seen as well. These apparitions I can verify from personal experience. When I was in elementary school, my family attended the Unitarian Universalist Fellowship on Blue Ridge Street, and me and my Sunday schoolmates would romp in the cemetery while the adults chatted after the sermon. One sunny spring afternoon, we were playing hide-and-seek, using the gravestones for cover. I saw an unfamiliar child in a suit jacket and short pants and shouted at him to hide before he was caught. To my dismay, he simply vanished. I ran to the spot to see if he was okay and saw only the marker of a child's grave. I sprinted back to church in hysterics. My parents wrote it off as an overactive imagination and too many ghost stories at a sitting. But I know what I saw and I don't want to see it again.

The story of the Tanning Yards is one of the more gruesome urban legends passed down by rural teens It begins with the rape and murder of a high school girl by a group of Satanists that lived in a farmhouse near the Norfolk Southern railway trestle. Her body was found in the creek under the rickety one-lane bridge nearby. When the police raided the house, no one was there and no evidence could tie the residents to the crime. No one ever knew the girl, which school she went to or when the crime was committed, but everyone knew someone who did know. The girl's ghost is reputed to walk in the creek from the house to the bridge as her screams of pain split the night air. Any car that just happened to be parked in the darkness under the trestle was fair game for her to climb into, begging all the while to be rescued.

When I was in college, the Tanning Yards was a popular spot to drink an underage beer or two or other high jinks. During my two years at Spartanburg Methodist, I spent about one day a week on average at the Tanning Yards and never had any odd experiences.

However, when I revisited the site as an adult to take some pictures, I did have a strange feeling on the trestle. I felt almost compelled to walk across the trestle to the other side of the creek in order to shoot the length of the creek. For whatever reason, I fought the urge and slid down the bank back to the car below. My friends Bill and Susan both asked what took me so long, and I explained the urge to them. About the time I finished, the roar and horn of a fast-moving freight train split the quiet. Based on prior experience, I estimated that I would have been halfway across about the time the train came out of the curve and bore down on me. The truly odd part of the whole experience is that there is a highway crossing less than a mile from the trestle and I never heard the train's horn at all.

Woodruff's Seven Devils Bridge: Finally, a bridge without a baby

Every once in a while a story just grabs your attention and makes you go find it on the ground. The hidden room in Glamis Castle in Scotland; the Devil's Stomping Ground in Siler City, North Carolina; and now, this lurid tale of a bridge that drives men insane joins this select group.

According to this legend, if you attempt to cross the bridge over Little Ferguson Creek at midnight, you will have a breakdown and cry and scream like a madman. No reason for this odd behavior is given.I found the bridge one evening while returning home from my parent's house. Just about midnight, I think it was, but I don't know for sure, I pulled over at the bridge. I was alone and briefly wondered how I would get home if I did have a breakdown but pushed on anyway. After a cigarette or two to settle my nerves, I started across. I stopped halfway and listened for any odd noises or out of place activity in the darkness. I saw no unexplainable lights or anything else strange, so I went on across. No nervous breakdown, no tears, not even a screaming fit. I walked slowly back across, cigarette number three at my lips, and still nothing. All I can say is either it wasn't my night or it was earlier than I thought, but nothing happened…to me anyway. As far as the name, no one I spoke to could tell me why they called the bridge "Seven Devils"; they just always have.

Walnut Lane Inn: Ashamed to admit I found it in a book

The good thing about doing a book like this is the sheer amount of things you did not know about places you thought you knew like the back of your hand. Take my hometown of Lyman for instance. My first ghost sighting happened on the railroad tracks near my great-grandparents' house. I was up there playing with some friends—you know, racing across the trestle over the Middle Tyger River and basically being "tween-age" boys. About dusk, we headed back to the house down the Norfolk Southern tracks when we saw a figure emerge from the brush behind us. We all first thought it was a local taking a shortcut to the nearby beer joint, until he reached the tracks. In the half-light we all realized at once that he had no head and was walking toward us. We bolted and reached home in what probably was record time. My father, who works for Norfolk Southern, knew of no wrecks or deaths on that part of the line. None of my great-grandparents' friends had heard anything about anyone being decapitated on the tracks, and most of them had lived in Lyman all their lives. It was and is a mystery. I have never seen him again, but the memory of the thrill that ran up my spine when I realized that I was seeing a real ghost has stayed with me ever since and is a major part of the reason for this book. But, I thought that would be the only ghost in Lyman. I was incorrect.

The Walnut Lane Inn is one of the landmarks in Lyman. Its large yard and two-story bulk is always a welcome sight on the long ride up to see my folks. I had no idea it was haunted, but it is, according to the book *Haunted Inns of America* by Terry Smith and Mark Jean. According to their account, there are at least two ghosts present at the inn, and possibly a third. The innkeeper, Hoyt Dottry, has seen two of his resident phantoms, one male and the other female. The male ghost appeared briefly in the kitchen, but no identification was possible. The second sighting was of a female in a dark skirt on the stairs. When followed, the lady simply vanished. Mr. Dottry believes she is the reason lampshades and pictures are often found tilted, despite being constantly straightened. The third ghost could be the same as the lady on the stairs, but she has not been seen, only heard. Mr. Dottry heard a woman's voice outside and then heard his dogs start barking, as if someone was nearby. No one was there or in the immediate area. I found no evidence of any deaths by violence on the site. I would recommend a visit anyway, as the inn is beautiful and convenient. The chance to see a ghost should merely be a bonus.

UNION COUNTY

Union County is in the central part of the Upstate and is surrounded by Cherokee, Spartanburg, Laurens, Newberry, Fairfield and Chester Counties. Union County was not a major Native American settlement prior to white settlement in the 1750s, as the area was mainly used as a hunting ground. The county was named for Union Church, which was founded in 1765 and served several congregations together.

The county was the site of five Revolutionary War battles, including Musgrove's Mill and Blackstock's, where General Thomas Sumter was wounded. Union County was not the site of any Civil War skirmishes, but Confederate President Jefferson Davis did spend the night in the town of Cross Keys with his cabinet on April 30, 1865. Union County was the home of three governors of South Carolina, though no US senators. One of the governors from Union County was William H. Gist, who served during the secession crisis of 1860. The other two governors were David Johnson and Thomas B. Jeter. The county seat is Union, which boasts a jail designed by Robert Mills, the designer of the Washington Monument.

The Inn at Merridun

The Inn at Merridun was built in the mid-1850s. Over the years, the Merriman, Rice and Duncan families called the property home, hence the name of the current inn. The property was placed on the National Register of Historical Places in 1974. According to legend, at least ten ghosts call Merridun home. As a result, this is probably the best-documented haunting in Union County. The tale has appeared in *Haunted Inns of the Southeast* by Shelia Turnage and *Haunted Inns of America* by Terry Smith and Mark Jean, as well as an article in the *Spartanburg Herald-Journal*.

The best-known ghosts at Merridun are T.C. and Fannie Duncan. The Duncans lived in the house in the late 1800s. T.C. Duncan served as a state senator from Union County and built the first cotton mill in the county. The Duncans most often manifest through the presence of two distinct scents, cigar smoke (smoking is not permitted in the inn) and an old-fashioned rose perfume. The couple is also believed to be the source of the scattering of pennies occasionally found in rooms that have just been cleaned.

There are many other hauntings at Merridun as well. A sister of one of the former residents has also been seen, but only from the neck down. Two children, assumed to be a brother and sister, have also made appearances. On occasion, the sound of Native American drumming has been heard in the night, as well as what is either harpsichord or piano music. No Native Americans currently live near the property, and the inn has no piano or harpsichord. A white dog has been seen both inside and outside the house and makes the innkeeper's cats rather unhappy when it pops up. The dog is seen with and without its presumed owner, a lady. I have not received clarification if this is the same lady who is rumored to "spoon" with guests, both male and female, on occasion. The final ghost reported at Merridun is that of an African American housekeeper, who has been seen doing chores outside the building. I have not stayed at the Inn at Merridun, so I can't offer any firsthand account of the hauntings, but I look forward to an opportunity to verify them for myself.

Juxa Plantation

Juxa Plantation is another haunted bed and breakfast found in Union County. This bed and breakfast is haunted by members of the Gregory family, the original owners of the plantation. The ghost is most often seen in the Gregory family cemetery on the property. The current owner believes the man she saw while doing yard work was Jehu Gregory, the patriarch of the family.

The cemetery had two grave markers that had been damaged over the passage of time and used in the construction of the former smokehouse. Since the stones were replaced in the cemetery, the ghost of Jehu Gregory has not made another appearance. However, auditory events have occurred inside the main house. The sounds of people arguing and singing have been heard in empty guest rooms. Light switches and pillows have also been messed with by someone who was not a paying guest or not visible to the naked eye. The Gregory family is allowed to hold a family reunion on the property, which is a nice gesture by the current owners in recognition of the family's role in the past of the county.

Cry baby bridge, Tyger River style

This version of the classic cry baby bridge legend is set on the Tyger River near Rose Hill State Park, the former plantation of Governor William Gist. This story is remarkably similar to the account found in Chester County. In the 1950s, a woman is said to have thrown her newborn off the bridge to spite her husband. As in Chester, if you park your car on the bridge and cut the engine off, you will hear the last cries of the baby and then see the mother looking over the edge of the bridge for the child.

My first visit to this bridge occurred by accident. Returning from a job interview at Rose Hill State Park in 1998, I took a wrong turn trying to get back to US 176 to Chester. It was early November, about seven o'clock, just after dusk. As soon as I saw the rusted steel frame of the bridge, I had a feeling that a ghost would be likely to pop up. At the time, I hadn't heard the legend about this particular bridge, but I played a hunch and parked in the center. Thankfully, there was no other traffic. Shortly after I cut my car off, I felt a distinct chill in the air and the usual background noise seemed to fade. I was roused from my stupor by the unmistakable sound of an unhappy baby. I got out of my car and leaned over the bridge and stared into the murky darkness below. Seeing nothing, I ran to the other side of the bridge and saw nothing. By this point, I knew I was hearing a ghost and decided not to wait around to see what else would develop. Not that I was frightened or anything...

Sadly, I could not locate the bridge when I went back in the spring of 2005. I tried every bridge between Rose Hill and US 176 and had no luck locating a steel-framed bridge anywhere.

Rose Hill State Park: More than a beautiful garden

The area around Rose Hill State Park itself has its own share of legends. These tales are depicted in an October 2004 article from the *Union Grapevine*, a free newsletter. One story concerns mysterious lights that appear in the nearby woods just after dawn. Hunters claim that the light resembles a man on horseback carrying a lantern. Those who have seen the light believe it is Governor Gist, still making his morning rounds. Since legend has it that his horse was buried next to him, it is possible that this figure is him and I can believe that he would still be interested in the state of affairs at his former home.

There is another story concerning the Gist family and the area around Rose Hill. Prior to the Civil War, one of Governor's Gist's daughters and a slave companion were out berry picking near what is now Sardis Road. A carriage came along and, for whatever reason, the horses were spooked. The daughter dove into the woods unharmed, but the slave girl was killed. Drivers along that road have reported seeing the two girls along the roadside, then witnessing the white child dive into the woods while the black girl vanishes.

Lake John D. Long
and the sorrow Susan Smith caused

The Susan Smith case shocked the nation in October 1994. For nine days, the young mother of two sons, Michael and Alex, stood by her story that she was the victim of a carjacking and that the boys had been abducted by a black male. The truth was even more shocking. Smith had strapped her sons into their car seats and sent her Mazda off of the boat ramp at Lake John D. Long with the boys inside.

Shortly after the reported kidnapping and continuing through Susan Smith's trial, the area near the dam at Lake Long became home to a makeshift memorial to the two young victims. This has since been replaced by a stone marker

After the trial, people visiting the site to pay their respects or simply to rubberneck began to report seeing two small balls of light hovering over the dam and moving slowly across the still water. Another odd event occurred in September 1996, when a van full of visitors rolled down the same ramp into the lake, drowning seven of the ten people present, including four children. According to local lore, the parking brake was engaged at the time the van rolled into the lake.

I have visited the site twice. My first visit in 1998 passed without incident. My second visit occurred in 2005. I arrived on a rainy March afternoon, thinking I would take a few photographs and then move on. Imagine my shock when two small balls of blue light floated over the dam and the deserted lake before me. I grabbed the camera and snapped two shots. The orbs did not appear on either shot, despite being visible to my naked eye. This is rather different from my usual experience, when the orbs show up on film and not to the naked eye.

The lake is open to the public for fishing, as is the infamous boat ramp.

Legends of Lockhart

Lockhart is best known as being one of the last "company-owned" mill villages in South Carolina. Milliken and Company sold the town and the Lockhart

Power Company to its residents in the late 1990s, after closing and demolishing the mill. The town is thriving and it is very easy on the eyes. It occupies a steep slope going down to the Broad River. It is also home to two ghostly legends.

The first story is centered at the Lockhart water tower. It concerns a lady in a white gown who is said to have leapt off the tower in the early twentieth century. She now dances around the tower's base with a rose in her mouth. She only appears at midnight, and if a witness does not compliment her on her dress, she will climb to the top of the tower and jump off, only to vanish before reaching the ground.

I have visited the site twice, once alone and before midnight, and once at midnight on Halloween in 2004. The long walk uphill over and around fallen trees was unremarkable, until the base of the tower became visible. A white mist hung around the base and the usual background noise one finds in the woods was not present. I waited for about ten minutes, until the sudden chill in the air became too much for me. I did not see anything. The Union County Library had no information on any suicides in Lockhart, and the tower appeared to have either been refurbished or replaced—it is likely that the ghost has finally found peace.

The second story in the Lockhart area is the source of some dispute. Sleepy Hollow Lane has been rumored to be haunted by a one-armed figure standing on the roadside crying for help. Legends differ on how he came to be there. The first theory is that the man was killed in the Civil War, but there is no evidence of any deaths in the area during that period. The second theory came from one of my friend Susan Hoff's coworkers and a native of the area. She claims the man is a local eccentric who was prone to harass passing motorists after losing an arm in an industrial accident. I have driven through the area at night and have not seen anyone on the side of the road, with or without a missing arm, but I urge those interested to check it out for themselves.

The Hound of Goshen revisited

The Hound of Goshen is one of the best-documented and longest-lasting ghost stories in the Upstate. It is also one of the few hauntings I have seen for myself more than once.

My second encounter with the Hound of Goshen occurred shortly after I started collecting tales for this book. I went out for a ride with the express intent of finding the hound. I felt that my chances were good, since it has been reported as recently as the late 1990s. I arrived on Maybinton Road about eight o'clock on a chilly February night. The news had threatened snow, which, with the prospect of seeing a ghost, had killed my wife's enthusiasm for the jaunt. So I was alone. After about two miles, I caught a glimpse of movement in the trees. After a few seconds, I saw a large white dog leap a ditch and head for my back bumper. I sped up to about fifty miles per hour, which is rather fast for a rural road in the winter, and glanced in my rear view mirror. To my excitement, the dog kept pace. I quickly found a driveway to turn around in and headed back toward it. The dog came forward at a good clip, only to vanish just before impact. Having hit a dog (and two deer), I know all too well that sickening thud. I braced for the impact that never came then sped off back to my apartment. I was thrilled to have seen the Hound again, but was unprepared for such excitement.

YORK
COUNTY

Y ork County is located in the northern part of the Upstate and is bordered by the state of North Carolina, and Lancaster, Chester, Union and Cherokee Counties. Native American activity in the area dates to at least 500 BC. The county is the homeland of the Catawba Indian tribe and is the site of the only federally recognized Indian reservation in South Carolina. By the late 1740s, white settlement had begun in the area, though some traders from Virginia passed through the area about 1650. By the mid-1770s, a small ironworking industry had developed in the area. The primary focus of the area, however, was trade. In 1772, the boundary between North and South Carolina was run and what is now York County was added to the state and called the New Acquisition District.

York County was the site of four Revolutionary War battles, including the battle of King's Mountain, which helped set the stage for the Yorktown campaign. York County was officially formed in 1785, though it lost part of its territory to Cherokee County in 1897. The county was named for York, England, by way of York, Pennsylvania. York County was the site of one minor action during the Civil War, when some Federal cavalry burned a railroad bridge over the Catawba River at Nations Ford in April 1865. York County did give one general to the Confederate cause, Micah Jenkins, who died at the Battle of the Wilderness in 1864. Jefferson Davis spent two nights in late April 1865 in York County and held his last formal cabinet meeting at the White family home near Fort Mill. At this meeting, Confederate Secretary of the Treasury G.A. Trenholm resigned and Postmaster General J.H. Reagan was named as his successor.

Following the defeat of the Confederacy, York County and its county seat, York, became hotbeds of Ku Klux Klan activity during Reconstruction. Rock Hill, the largest city in the county, was the site of sit-ins by students at Friendship (now Clinton) Junior College in 1959 and 1960 at a local department store. These sit-ins led to the "jail, no bail" protests that eventually led to the peaceful integration of downtown shopping. In 1961, future US Representative John Lewis from Georgia was attacked and beaten while passing through Rock Hill as a Freedom Rider.

The area is fast-growing due to its proximity to Charlotte, North Carolina.

Ben Tillman (and others) wander Winthrop University

Ben Tillman was governor and a senator from South Carolina, but his influence went far beyond the offices he held. He was an agrarian, a racist and a rabble-rouser, as witnessed by his nickname, "Pitchfork." He got this nickname while running for the US Senate in 1894, when he threatened to stick a pitchfork in "Old Grover's" (President Cleveland's) ribs if sent to Washington. Tillman was one of the driving forces behind the introduction of Jim Crow restrictions and voting limits on African Americans. He was also one of the leaders in the introduction of women's higher education in South Carolina, as evidenced by his concern for (some would say micromanagement of) Winthrop University in Rock Hill.

Tillman's portrait hangs at the entrance of Tillman Hall, the main administrative building on campus. Most say that the portrait's one eye follows visitors all over the ground floor. (Tillman lost an eye to a disease as a child.) Some people claim his ghost is trapped in the portrait, but others say he roams the old tunnels under the campus or stays in the bell tower of Tillman Hall. Most sightings have occurred on the second floor in front and in the auditorium. People claim to see a tall man in an old-fashioned black suit walking away from them. Witnesses are frozen in their tracks when the man turns and looks just like the portrait downstairs.

Those who believe he still lurks the halls date his existence to the revision of the strict holiday policy he had installed while he was governor and the anger and stress that caused him. I have not seen Senator Tillman, but his portrait is a disconcerting sight upon arrival on campus, and it does seem to track you on the first floor.

However, during my year as graduate assistant in the history department at Winthrop, I occasionally had to deliver intercampus mail. The mail was picked up in the basement of Tillman Hall. One spring day, after dropping something off at the cashier's office, I headed up the hall. I was alone until I saw a shirtless figure carrying a load of lumber. Being rather full of myself, I decided to advise him on proper dress in a campus building. Just as I drew level with him, the man walked through a bricked-up doorframe. Shortly after I regained my self-control, I realized the man was a large black man who was both shirtless and shoeless. I can only imagine that he was one of the convict laborers who had died during the building's construction.

Other ghosts at Winthrop include a former student searching for her room in her former dorm, Margaret Nance Hall, and a former professor who rattles locked doorknobs in a girls' dorm, Lee Wicker Hall. The young woman in search of her room died in a car crash off campus, but I have not heard any reason for the professor's return.

Historic Brattonsville

Historic Brattonsville is a living history farm and was the site of the Revolutionary Battle of Huck's Defeat, in which a local Tory leader was killed while harassing the matriarch of the patriot Bratton family. Nearly a century later, one member of the family, Dr. Rufus Bratton, fled Federal troops to Canada at the height of Klan activity in York and was forcibly returned to face trial. Dr. Bratton is believed to be one of the inspirations for Thomas Dixon's novel *The Clansman*, which was the basis for the film *Birth of a Nation*.

Today the Historic Brattonsville site is home to reenactments of the famous Revolutionary War battle, as well as "slave" interpreters and other representations of the history of the county and the Bratton family. There are also two ghosts connected with the area.

One legend focuses on the old slave cemetery. A slave named Watt, who reportedly warned Colonel Bratton that the Tory force under Captain Huck was approaching the plantation, and his wife are buried there in marked graves. People have reported seeing a shadowy figure in the surrounding woods about dusk. No one has gotten a good clear look at the figure, but it is believed to be Watt. I have been in the area at the appropriate time and seen something in the woods, but I can not say what exactly. The other manifestations have occurred near the restored blacksmith's shop. Visitors have reported hearing voices and had feelings of being watched, though no one was nearby. Sounds of metal banging and rhythmic hammering and lights in an unoccupied building have also been observed. On my visits, I have not had any odd experiences, but I feel that with as much life as has passed through Brattonsville, a ghost would not be a real surprise. A slave-life interpreter at Historic Brattonsville, Mozell Robinson, told me that she has worked there for years at various times of the day, both early morning and late at night, and has never had any unusual experiences.

Red River Road: Really odd goings-on

Red River Road is less than a mile from I-77 and runs next to a major industrial site in Rock Hill. It also runs very near a major commercial area. The area was developed as a textile mill in the 1920s and has been placed on the National Register of Historical Places in 1991. However, this busy road is home to many strange sightings and occurrences. People have reported taking photographs of and inside several abandoned houses near Lynderboro Road, which is a side street off of Red River Road, that all come out distorted when developed. There have also been reports of a satanic church in the area, and people claim to experience odd feelings there.

I have driven through the area several dozen times at all hours, as it is a good bypass for the Interstate during construction, accidents or other delays. I have also been on Lynderboro Road looking around, but I have never felt uncomfortable there, whatever the time of day (or night). Since I don't trespass, I haven't been in any of the abandoned houses and have not taken any photographs in the area. Perhaps these tales are simply urban legends, but nonetheless there are some very strange things happening on Red River Road.

Major Ferguson *still* doesn't like Americans

Kings Mountain was one of the major battles of the Revolution and one of the few clear-cut patriot victories, even if it did come against mainly fellow Americans and not regular British troops. Major Patrick Ferguson, the Tory commander, was the only Briton (he was a Scot) to fight at Kings Mountain. He earned a small share of fame for designing a breech-loading rifle and for refusing to shoot General George Washington in the back at the Battle of Brandywine. Major Ferguson also served to galvanize patriot opposition in the backcountry areas of North and South Carolina and what is now Tennessee after the patriot defeats at Charleston and Camden. He sent out a proclamation urging submission to the British Crown or he would "hang their leaders and lay their country to waste with fire and sword." Some nine hundred hand-picked sharpshooters, under Colonels Isaac Shelby, John Sevier, William McDowell and William Campbell, met up with the eleven hundred Loyalist militia under Ferguson at King's Mountain on October 7, 1780. What followed was a crushing defeat for the British cause in America, as General Cornwallis lost his left flank and staggered to final surrender at Yorktown, Virginia, just over a year later.

Ferguson was the only mounted officer on the field, as the patriot colonels dismounted to charge with their troops up the slopes, using boulders and trees for cover. He wore a blue tartan jacket and held his sword in his left hand due to an elbow injury on his right arm. His men were unfortified on a bare ridge and shooting downhill toward foes who knew how to use cover. Ferguson had personally cut down several white flags, and the actions of his colleague Banastre Tarleton at earlier battles in the Upstate—especially at Buford's Massacre in Lancaster County— made the patriots even less inclined to allow the Loyalists to surrender easily. The result was a massacre. The Loyalists lost almost 1,000 men: 225 killed, 123 wounded and 716 captured The patriots lost less than 100 men, 28 dead and 64 wounded. Ferguson fell with dozens of bullets in his body and his corpse was stripped and urinated on by his conquerors. The urinating on his grave was a mark of the disrespect these men had for Ferguson. However, the patriot commanders did finally give him a decent burial under a cairn of stones in order to prevent animals from disturbing the remains.

The haunting at Kings Mountain is multifaceted. Campers and reenactors have often complained to rangers that they have heard people walking and riding through the woods, despite posted warnings to remain on the paved path, and have claimed to hear gunfire in the thick woods that surround the walking trail. Some people have seen a figure with a "disgustingly smug" smile on his face near Ferguson's cairn or seen a flash of blue fade into the woods at dusk. The figure only appears at dusk and always bears the same expression. Occasionally he has been known to laugh and dispute the effectiveness of the Scotch-Irish traditions of using urine on a fresh grave or building a cairn in order to keep a corpse from wandering before vanishing. Robert Dunkerly, a ranger at the park and the author of the *Kings Mountain Walking Tour Guide*, told me in a March 2005 interview that he has never seen or heard anything unusual at the site, despite being there at odd hours at times. He did share some experiences that other people had told him over the years. One camper was sleeping near the battle monument on top of the ridge when he was poked by invisible hands. The man stayed awake all night with his back to the monument and left at first light. Another camper told of meeting a group of men wearing period clothes on the trail. He raised his reproduction lantern to guide the lightless men, only to have his own light blown out. As soon as he relit the light, he was alone on the paved path.

My most recent visit to Kings Mountain was in March 2005. I walked up to the US monument and stopped by Ferguson's cairn and his monument. It was about four o'clock in the afternoon, and I did not have any unusual experiences. However, on my previous visit to the site, while I was in graduate school, I walked the entire 1.5-mile trail loop. About three-quarters of the way around, while on my way up to the battle monument, dusk began to settle in. I picked up my pace, as I had been leisurely strolling and taking advantage of the rainy weather to have the park to myself, only to be brought up short by an indistinct voice off to my right up the slope. I had not heard the stories about the park being haunted at that point, but I swear I thought I heard someone whisper, "Get down."

Fort Mill High School

In many ways, this story is the perfect one to end this book with. The story is simple. At midnight on Friday the thirteenth at Fort Mill High School in Fort Mill, every locker is supposedly emptied and the contents are scattered all over the school. Over the course of the school day, the lights are said to flicker on and off. This is reputed to be the warning of the ghost. According to the legend, the school was built over a graveyard.

I called the school on a Friday the thirteenth in 2005 and asked if anything had happened. The secretary I spoke to almost choked during her laughing fit while saying no. She had heard the rumors of a ghostly visit but told me that nothing unusual had happened. When I checked back on Monday the sixteenth, the story was the same.

I asked the York County Library if they had any information on any cemeteries being damaged during the school's construction. They told me no and the information in the Chester County Library collection verified that report. However, as with many other legends and hauntings, there could be more to the story, and I leave to you to decide if there is.

BIBLIOGRAPHY

Books

Asfar, Dan. *Haunted Battlefields.* Edmonton, Alberta: Ghost House Books, 2004.

Ballard, Mignon. *Cry at Dusk: A Novel of Suspense.* New York: Dodd, Mead, and Company, 1987.

Barefoot, Daniel. *Haunted Halls of Ivy: Ghosts of Southern Colleges and Universities.* Winston-Salem, North Carolina: John F. Blair, 2004.

Bolick, Julian. *A Fairfield Sketchbook.* Clinton, South Carolina: Jacobs Brothers, 1963.

Brasington, JoAnn Mitchell. *The South Carolina School for the Deaf and Blind: 1849–1999.* Spartanburg, South Carolina: privately printed, 2000.

Catawba Regional Planning Council. *Historic Sites Survey: Chester County.* n.p. 1976.

———. *Historic Sites Survey: Lancaster County.* n.p. 1976.

———. *Historic Sites Survey: Union County.* n.p. 1976.

———. *Historic Sites Survey: York County.* n.p. 1976.

Chester District Genealogical Society. *Tombstone Inscriptions: Evergreen Cemetery, Chester, South Carolina.* Baltimore: Gateway Press, 2004.

Collins, Anne. *A Goodly Heritage: History of Chester County South Carolina.* Columbia, South Carolina: R.L. Bryan, 1986.

BIBLIOGRAPHY

Dunkerly, Robert. *Kings Mountain Walking Tour Guide.* Pittsburgh: Dorrance, 2003.

Egerton, John. *Speak Now Against the Day: The Generation before the Civil Rights Movement in the South.* New York: Knopf, 1994.

Feaster, Mrs. W.F. *A History of Union County, South Carolina.* Greenville, South Carolina: A Press, Inc., 1977.

Hauck, Dennis. *Haunted Places: The National Directory: Ghostly Abodes, Sacred Sites, UFO Landings, and Other Supernatural Locations.* New York: Penguin, 2002.

Knox, Louise Gill. *Chester's History and Architecture on the Hill.* Chester, South Carolina, privately printed, 1986.

Lipscomb, Terry. *Battles, Skirmishes, and Actions of the American Revolution in South Carolina.* Columbia, South Carolina: South Carolina Department of Archives and History, 1991.

McMillan, Montague. *Limestone College: A History, 1845–1970.* Gaffney, South Carolina: Limestone College, 1970.

Roberts, Nancy. *Ghosts and Specters of the Old South: Ten Supernatural Stories.* Orangeburg, South Carolina: Sandlapper, 1984.

———. *Ghosts of the Carolinas.* Columbia, South Carolina: University of South Carolina Press, 1967.

———. *South Carolina Ghosts: From the Coast to the Mountains.* Columbia, South Carolina: University of South Carolina Press, 1983.

Smith, Terry L., and Mark Jean. *Haunted Inns of America: National Directory of Haunted Hotels and Bed and Breakfast Inns.* Crane Hill, 2003.

Stauffer, Michael. *The Formation of Counties in South Carolina.* Columbia, South Carolina: Department of Archives and History, 1994.

Summer, G. Leland. *Folklore of South Carolina, Including Central and Dutch Fork Sections of the State, and Much Data on the Early Quaker and Covenanter Customs, Etc.* Copy in S. Lewis Bell Collection, Chester County Library.

Toney, B. Keith. *Battlefield Ghosts.* Berryville, Virginia: Rockbridge Publishing, 1997.

Turnage, Shelia. *Haunted Inns of the Southeast.* Winston-Salem, North Carolina: John F. Blair, 2001.

Vandiver, Louise Ayer. *Traditions and History of Anderson County.* Atlanta: Ruralist Press, 1928.

Workers of the Writers' Program of the Work Projects Administration in the State of South Carolina. *Palmetto Place Names: Their Origins and Meanings.* Columbia, South Carolina: South Carolina Education Association, n.d.

———. *South Carolina: A Guide to the Palmetto State.* American Guide Series. New York: Oxford University Press, 1941.

BIBLIOGRAPHY

Zepke, Terrance. *Best Ghost Tales of South Carolina*. Sarasota, Florida: Pineapple Press, 2004.

Articles

Alongi, Paul. "Fire Races through Abandoned Hospital." *Greenville (SC) News*. November 20, 2002.

Bigham, John. "Chester Names." *Names in South Carolina* (University of South Carolina, Columbia, English Department) 29 (Winter 1982), 31–33.

Boyanoski, John. "Upstate Rich with Legends of Ghosts and Haunted Buildings." *Greenville (SC) News*. October 29, 2003.

Dean, Suellen. "Ghosts Welcome at Inn." *Spartanburg (SC) Herald-Journal*. October 31, 1994.

Fant, Christie. "Historic Landmarks in Lexington and Newberry Counties.". *Names in South Carolina* 28 (Winter, 1981), 45–51.

"Halloween in Union County." *Union (SC) Grapevine*. October 2004.

Hewell, Marion. "Some Greenville Names." *Names in South Carolina* 10 (Winter, 1963), 24–28.

Jenkins, Alan. "Ghost Hunter and the Little Theater." *News and Reporter* (Chester, South Carolina). July 21, 2004.

Johnson, Tally. "Theater or Specter?" *News and Reporter* (Chester, South Carolina). October 29, 2004.

"Madeline—The Legend." *Newberry College…Where People Make It Special* (Newberry College, Newberry, South Carolina). October 29, 1986.

Neuffer, Claude Henry. "Four Year Colleges." *Names in South Carolina* 22 (Winter, 1975), 29–33.

Nutt, Karen. "Upstate Has Share of Ghosts, Goblins." *Spartanburg (SC) Herald-Journal*. October 27, 1994.

Orr, Susan. "Ghosts in the Hall." *Spartanburg (SC) Herald-Journal*. October 29, 2000.

Pegram, W.W. "Explosion Wrecks Telephone Office." *Chester (SC) News*. July 18, 1932.

Pettibon, Sula. "Students Aren't the Only Souls Haunting Winthrop's Halls." *Rock Hill (SC) Herald*. August 24, 2004.

Shannon, James. "The Haunting of the Upstate." *Greenville (SC) MetroBEAT*. October 20, 2004.

"Students Hear Ghost Playing Piano at Night." *Echoes* (Anderson College, Anderson, South Carolina). November 19, 1987.

White, Marissa. "Crybaby Bridge and Other Chester County Tales of Terror." *Chester (SC) News and Reporter*. October 29, 2003.

Woodcock, Julie. "Gaffney Strangler." *Spartanburg (SC) Herald-Journal*. February 8, 2000.

Personal Interviews

Addison, Alice. Eyewitness to Chester Little Theater haunting. Interview with the author. April 8, 2005.

Bowen, Lisa. Eyewitness to Walker Hall haunting. Interview with the author. South Carolina School for the Deaf and Blind, Spartanburg, South Carolina, June 20, 2005.

Bramlett, Nikki. Eyewitness to Chester Little Theater haunting. Interview with the author. November 10, 2004.

Carter, Jane. Secretary, Bethel United Methodist Church, Chester, South Carolina. Phone interview with the author. April 25, 2005.

Cathcart, Lisa. Fairfield County local historian. Phone interview with the author. March 16, 2005.

Clayton, Chris. Custodian, Chester Associate Reformed Presbyterian Church. Interview with the author. May 3, 2005.

Craig, Melody. Lancaster County local historian. Phone interview with the author. March 16, 2005.

Dubose, Brenda. Anderson College library employee. E-mail exchange with the author. January 2005.

Dunkerly, Robert. Ranger, Kings Mountain National Military Park. Interview with the author. Kings Mountain National Military Park. March 20, 2005.

Feaster, Billy. Chester County Library employee. Interview with the author. May 27, 2005.

Gunsallus, David. Pickens County Library employee. E-mail exchange with the author. May 2005.

Harris, Gary. Lancaster County Library employee. E-mail exchange with the author. February 2005.

Holden, Laura. Anderson County Library employee. E-mail exchange with the author. February 2005.

Kubias, Craig. Limestone College chaplain. Phone interview with the author. March 14, 2005.

Long, Melinda Brown. Teacher at Tanglewood Middle School, Greenville, South Carolina. E-mail exchange with the author. April 2005.

McCall, Bob. Oconee County Library employee. E-mail exchange with the author. April 2005.

Price-Coleman, Glinda. Director, Great Falls Hometown Association. Phone interview with the author. April 11, 2005.

Roddey, Bill. Former student at Spartanburg Methodist College. Interview with the author. February 12, 2005.

Roddey, John. Eyewitness to haunting at Chester Little Theater. Interview with the author. October 21, 2004.

Slayton, Becky. Administrator, Walnut Grove Plantation, Moore, South Carolina. E-mail exchange with the author. January 2005.

Sloan, Lawrence. Former student and employee at South Carolina School for the Deaf and Blind, Spartanburg, South Carolina. Interview with the author (through sign language interpreter). South Carolina School for the Deaf and Blind, Spartanburg, South Carolina. June 20, 2005.

Stone-Wylder, Stavia. Eyewitness to Bethel UMC haunting. Interview with the author. April 20, 2005.

Tinker, Linda. Secretary, Chester ARP Church. Interview with the author. May 3, 2005.

Washko, Mary. Employee of South Carolina School for the Deaf and Blind, Spartanburg, South Carolina. Interview with the author (through sign language interpreter). South Carolina School for the Deaf and Blind, Spartanburg, South Carolina. June 20, 2005.

Wellington, Roger. Employee of Greenville County Library. E-mail exchange with the author. March 2005.

Wylder, John. Former employee, Spartanburg Technical College Library. E-mail exchange with the author. February 2005.

Wylie, Anita. Eyewitness to haunting on Henry Woods Lane, Chester, South Carolina. Interview with the author. January 17, 2005.

Wylie, Jessica. Eyewitness to haunting at Chester Little Theater. Interview with the author. March 23, 2005.

Websites

South Carolina Ghosthunters Forums. http://www.scghosthunters.com/

The Shadowlands, Ghosts & Hauntings. http://www.theshadowlands.net/ghost/

Southern Ghost Stories. http://southcarolinaghost.tripod.com/GhostStories/

Visit us at:
www.historypress.net